Finding the Jesus Experience

Real Life...
Real Questions...
REAL JESUS

χ The Greek Way to Say Jesus

For centuries it has been a symbol for Christ, the anointed one, the Savior. First-century Christians used the Greek letter χ (pronounced ki or key), which is the first letter in the Greek word for Christ, χριστός (pronounced Kree-stas) as a shorthand for Jesus. The χ quickly became incorporated into a variety of symbols to represent early Christians' faith in the one God sent, Jesus. It was simple. It pointed to the cross and became a sign identifying believers. The mark and its variation can be found in ancient Roman catacombs, early coins, lamps, and pottery.

Today, χ still stands for Christ. It is the bridge between the countless number of Christ-followers through history to a new millennium. As you prepare yourself for the future, you will need the right tools to make sense of a world that often appears senseless. You will need answers to the tough questions. You will need a firm foundation on which to make good decisions about your life and your future. You will need the χ—Jesus.

Through this devotional, *Finding the Jesus Experience*, and its companion devotional books, *Knowing the Real Jesus, Meeting the Jesus Challenge*, and *Discovering the Jesus Answers*, you will encounter the *real* Jesus and what he has to say about faith, pain and suffering, relationships, and other issues that touch your life. In this series of 30 devotions, you will discover who Jesus really is, why he came to earth, and why he deserves your trust, your worship, and your faith.

χ. One symbol. One hope. One man. One God. One Truth. It's all you'll ever need.

Finding the Jesus Experience

Real Life...
Real Questions...
REAL JESUS

Linda Washington

EMPOWERED® Youth Products

Standard Publishing
Cincinnati, Ohio

All Scripture quotations, unless otherwise indicated, are taken from the *Holy Bible,* New Living Translation, copyright © 1996. Used by permission of Tyndale House Publishers, Inc., Wheaton, IL 60189. All rights reserved.

Developed and produced for Standard Publishing by The Livingstone Corporation. Project staff includes: Kirk Luttrell, Andrea Reider, Betsy Todt Schmitt, Ashley Taylor, and David R. Veerman.

Some material included in *Finding the Jesus Experience* was used by permission from *The Jesus Bible,* copyright ©2002 by Tyndale House Publishers, Inc. All rights reserved.

Contributing writers include: Mark Fackler, Amber Hudson, Randy Southern, Linda Washington, and Neil Wilson.

Standard Publishing development and editorial team includes: Paul Learned, Darrell Lewis, Dale Reeves, acquisitions editor, and Mark Taylor.

Cover design, Ahaa! Design

Interior design, Kirk Luttrell, The Livingstone Corporation

Library of Congress Cataloging-in-Publication Data:
Washington, Linda M., 1960-
     Finding the Jesus experience / Linda Washington.
        p. cm. – (Real life–real questions–real Jesus)
     ISBN 0-7847-1421-5 (pbk.)
        1. Youth–Prayer-books and devotions–English. 2. Emotions–Religious aspects–Christianity–Meditations. 3. Interpersonal relations–Religious aspects–Christianity–Meditations. I. Title. II. Series.
     BV4850 .W319 2002
     242'.634–dc21   2002008140

EMPOWERED® Youth Products is a trademark of Standard Publishing.

Printed in the United States of America.

Standard Publishing, Cincinnati, Ohio.

A Division of Standex International Corporation.

09	08	07	06	05	04	03	02
7	6	5	4	3	2	1	

Contents

The Jesus Experience

The *Real Life . . . Real Questions . . . Real Jesus* series, consisting of four devotional books and four leader's guides for youth leaders, were written as companion pieces to *The Jesus Bible.* This Bible, published by Tyndale Publishing House and produced and developed by The Livingstone Corporation, was designed to help introduce the Jesus of the Bible to you in a new and fresh way. *The Jesus Bible* follows the work and purpose of Christ from the Old Testament prophecies about him to his life and ministry on earth. It records Jesus' call to radical living, first voiced about 2,000 years ago, that still resounds today.

Through the features and notes found in *The Jesus Bible,* you will encounter Jesus in ways you have never experienced before—not the watered-down religious pacifist or the timid-looking person in a stained-glass window. But the Christ, the Messiah, the Savior, the real Jesus—in all his color, with all his power, showing up in the most unexpected places and taking the most revolutionary actions. Through *The Jesus Bible,* you will meet the real Jesus for real life with real answers for life's tough problems.

Why the New Living Translation?

Since its inception, Tyndale House Publishing has been committed to publishing editions of the Bible in the language of the common people. With more than 40 million copies in print, *The Living Bible* represented this tradition for more than 30 years. In recent years, Tyndale continued its commitment and mission by commissioning 90 evangelical scholars to produce the *Holy Bible,* New Living Translation. This general-purpose translation is accurate and excellent for study, yet it is easy to read and understand.

The team of translators was challenged to create a text that would have the same impact in the lives of modern readers as the original text did in the lives of early believers. To accomplish that, the team translated entire thoughts (rather than just words) into natural, everyday

English. The result is a translation that speaks to us today in our language, a translation that is easy to understand, and that accurately communicates the meaning of the original texts.

In using the New Living Translation for *The Jesus Bible* and in the *Real Life . . . Real Questions . . . Real Jesus* series, the publishers at Tyndale House and Standard Publishing pray that this translation will speak to your heart and help you understand the Word of God in a fresh and powerful way.

Because you have real questions . . .
and Jesus has real answers!

Relationships. Everybody's got 'em. (Duh!) You can't live on this earth without having a relationship of some kind. Some relationships you're born into. Others—those with friends, for instance—you choose yourself. Even though you didn't choose your mom or your Uncle Fred, you can choose *how* you relate to each person. Some relationships will be deeper than others of course, unless you're the kind of person who has nothing but really, really close family and friends. ("I'd like to thank my two thousand best friends for this award.")

RELATIONSHIPS

The way you relate in any relationship comes from your experience with Jesus—how much you understand his love for you. Want to know how non-Christians should tell who the Christians are? Love. Love, according to Jesus, should be the hallmark of his followers (John 13:35).

The fact that we have relationships at all can be traced back to God. He created us to enjoy relationships. ("It is not good for the man to be alone"—Genesis 2:18.) Because God loves us, we can love others. That's the truth, plain and simple. You don't even need to read any further. Just kidding!

Just like snowflakes, no two relationships are the same. They're all unique. But some relationships share characteristics in common. Some might bring you more joy than others. Others might seem more trouble than they're worth. One thing is for sure: all relationships take work. And every once in a while, you might need a word or two of advice. Where can you get the help you need to handle your relationships? The Bible is a manual for relationships. If you're a believer, you also have a built-in advice counselor you can access quicker than Dr. Laura. He's the Holy Spirit.

God wants to do more than just hear about your relationships. He wants to be involved in them. Want to experience Jesus in your relationships? Read on.

DAY 1

I find the Jesus Experience when I let go of my expectations of others.

But the Lord said to her, "My dear Martha, you are so upset over all these details! There is really only one thing worth being concerned about. Mary has discovered it—and I won't take it away from her."

Luke 10:41-42

REAL Xpressions

Disappointment

My mama disappointed me again. She said she was going to come to my game but didn't show. That's my mama for you. She's good at saying, "My baby's going to be a basketball star someday." That's just what she told everybody when I made the team at my high school. But I can count on one finger the amount of times Mama has seen me play.

It's not every day that I start. I even hit double digits tonight. Twelve points! I was in a zone I guess. Anyway, everybody was congratulating me afterward. I looked up at the bleachers hoping that maybe Mama showed. Nope. She called me on the cell phone that she got me for my birthday to tell me she had to work late again.

That's the way it always is. She has to work late. I used to get mad about it and try to make her feel guilty. I'd bring up the fact that since my father left (when they divorced, he split; don't know where he is), at least my mama should come out and support me.

When I went to youth church on Sunday, I guess I was pouting about it or something. The youth pastor asked me what was up. When I told him, he got this funny look on his face and told me to read 1 Corinthians 13:4-7. Then he told me that I shouldn't keep trying to make Mama feel guilty just to get my own way. "Especially after all the things your mother does for you," he added, which made *me* feel guilty. I was determined *not* to read that passage. But since it stayed on my mind, I thought that maybe God wanted me to read it.

So, I read it. Talk about feeling low. It was all about what love was and wasn't. Verse five just jumped out at me. "Love does not demand its own way. Love is not irritable, and it keeps no record of when it has been wronged." Oops. I guess I've been taking stuff out on her.

Yeah, Mama disappointed me again. She wasn't there for me at the game. But at least she's there 24/7. I'm thankful for that.

Jalyn

REAL QUESTION

Would Jesus say that we're entitled to have all of our expectations met in our relationships?

We all have preconceived ideas of some kind or other about our relationships. Some expectations are realistic. Others aren't. Many of them are unspoken. Maybe we expect relationships to always work out or to meet our needs in some way. Maybe we expect relationships to be 50-50, with each person contributing half.

If we're honest, we might even have an expectation or two about the way we relate to God. Maybe we sometimes see him the way that Jalyn sees her mom—as someone who disappoints occasionally.

When our dreams aren't met, disappointment is the result. What did Jalyn count on from her mother? Was her mother able to meet her expectations? How realistic is Jalyn's expectation? Do you have a similar expectation from a parent or a friend?

REAL ANSWER

Jesus dealt with the expectations of others in unexpected ways. He often hung out at the home of his friends Mary, Martha, and Lazarus. (See Luke 10:38-42.) During one of those times, Martha became angry with her sister Mary for not doing her share of the work. Instead of helping, Mary sat at Jesus' feet listening to him. When Martha complained to Jesus, she probably expected him to take her side. Guess what? He didn't. Instead, he told her that Mary had chosen what was most important.

As the Messiah, Jesus didn't perform in a way that the people of Israel anticipated. He came to serve, rather than to be served (see Matthew 20:28).

He did what his Father wanted, rather than what *he* wanted. He didn't come as a conquering hero; he came as a humble carpenter.

Jesus never said that we would never be disappointed in life. But he did say this: "Your heavenly Father already knows all your needs, and he will give you all you need from day to day if you live for him and make the Kingdom of God your primary concern" (Matthew 6:32-33). Want to choose what's most important? "Make the Kingdom of God your primary concern." That might mean letting go of unrealistic expectations. It might just mean releasing your need to have your own way.

REAL YOU

I need to take an honest look at my expectations for my relationships. I'll start with the following relationship:

_____

_____

_____

_____

_____

_____

_____

_____

_____

_____

_____

_____

_____

_____

_____

_____

_____

_____

_____

_____

_____

_____

One thing I expect concerning my relationship with God is this:

_____

_____

_____

_____

_____

_____

_____

_____

_____

_____

_____

_____

_____

_____

_____

_____

_____

Xalted

Advocate

Need a lawyer—someone to
plead your defense? That's what an
advocate is. He or she is on your side.
First John 2:1 describes Jesus as our advocate.
Some relationships can cause you to feel misunderstood, hurt, or disappointed. If so, don't worry. You
have someone who is on your side. When you get stuck trying to deal with a relationship, take it to your heavenly Advocate.
He'll help you.

DaY 2

I find the Jesus Experience when I honor and respect my parents.

Then he [Jesus] returned to Nazareth with them and was obedient to them; and his mother stored all these things in her heart. So Jesus grew both in height and in wisdom, and he was loved by God and by all who knew him.

Luke 2:51-52

REAL Xpressions

True Love

Have you ever been so convinced that someone is right for you that you didn't even want to hear anyone else's opinion? I was that way about Shemar. I met him six months ago at a party at my friend Jenice's house. Shemar is Jenice's cousin. We talked for a long time at the party. He didn't ask me out right away—not until he called me later on that week. I didn't know how old he was at the time. I kept asking him what school he went to. I thought maybe he was in college or something. He finally told me that he was twenty-five! I'm sixteen. Still, I thought I could handle the age difference.

There was only one tiny problem—Mama and my stepfather. (I call him "Pops.") When Shemar came to pick me up for our first date, I didn't tell them how old he was. All they knew was that he was Jenice's cousin. But they acted like they thought something was up. When I got home, Mama asked why he didn't talk about school. I casually mentioned that he was "older." She raised an eyebrow and nailed me. "How much older?" So I told her. She had a fit!

Pops wanted to know why someone Shemar's age wanted to date a teenager. Like I wasn't mature enough or something. Mama and Pops wanted me to break up with him. I didn't want to. I thought I was in love with Shemar. So home was like World War III for a while. I knew I needed to pray. Deep down, I knew that my attitude was wrong. I just wasn't ready to admit it! Finally, I talked to my friend Bonita about Shemar after church one Sunday. I was surprised (and kind of mad) when she sided with Mama and Pops! Then she brought up something she read in a devotional that morning. Even though we disagree with our parents, we still owe them respect. Well, I did *not* want to hear that! But eventually, God got through to me. I hadn't shown much respect to Mama and Pops. I knew it was time that I did.

Tasha

REAL QUESTION

Does Jesus really expect
you to respect your parents
even when you disagree with them?
At times, respecting parents might seem
like a pat answer that adults throw your way
when they can't think of anything better to say. Have
you ever felt that way?

Tasha disagreed with her mother and stepfather about
her choice of a boyfriend. They felt that he was too old, but she
disagreed. After all, she was in love—or thought she was. She even disagreed with her friend because her friend sided with her parents. Would
you give up your relationship with someone you cared about if your parents said no to it? Do you think you have to grit your teeth and be phony
when it comes to showing respect? Do you always have to "feel" respect-
ful in order to show respect?

REAL ANSWER

Samson—you know, the
guy with the hair problem—
didn't see any need to listen to his
parents about the women in his life. After
seeing a Philistine woman that he wanted to
marry, he told his parents, "Get her for me" even
though they objected to her. (See Judges 14:1-3.) They
didn't disapprove of his choice just because they felt like it.
They protested because they knew the marriage was against
God's law. But Samson didn't care. When it came to women, he usually
made the wrong choice. Later, he met a woman named Delilah. You know
what happened then!

Jesus, however, provides us with a completely different model—with
a completely different outcome. He was obedient to his parents. (See Luke
2:51.) One day his parents lost track of him during a trip back to Nazareth
from Jerusalem. When they found him talking to the leaders in the temple, they were a little upset with him. He didn't pull rank and say "Hey,
I'm the Son of God! I don't have to listen to you!" Instead, he humbly sub-
mitted to them. He knew that they wanted what was best for him.

Is this always easy? No. Sometimes being obedient might seem like that terrible-tasting medicine that you have to swallow. But knowing that they want what's best for you can help. And, if it's good enough for the Son of God, shouldn't it be good enough for you?

God commands his followers to honor their parents. (See Exodus 20:12; Ephesians 6:1-3.) He didn't put a condition on the command, for example: "respect them only if they're fair or you agree with them." He just said to respect them—period. By doing so, you honor God too.

REAL YOU

Because I'm a follower of Jesus, I need to obey my parents in the following area:

_____

_____

_____

_____

_____

_____

_____

_____

_____

_____

_____

_____

_____

_____

_____

_____

_____

_____

_____

_____

_____

_____

One area of my life in which my parents' advice doesn't make sense is . . .
Lord, help me to understand.

_____

_____

_____

_____

_____

_____

_____

_____

_____

_____

_____

_____

_____

_____

_____

_____

_____

XALTED

Master

God has put lots of people in
authority over you—parents, teachers,
pastors, policemen, government leaders—
and unless they tell you to sin, you should
obey them. (Check out Jude 1:4.) But ultimately,
you need to remember God has given them their
authority, and he alone is in charge over you and them.
Obeying them means that you're submitting to him as your Master.

DAY I find the Jesus Experience when I choose not to take revenge when someone hurts me.

"You have heard that the law of Moses says, 'If an eye is injured, injure the eye of the person who did it. If a tooth gets knocked out, knock out the tooth of the person who did it.' But I say, don't resist an evil person! If you are slapped on the right cheek, turn the other, too."

Matthew 5:38-39

REAL Xpressions

Idle Rumors

I couldn't believe it when I heard what Maria had said about me. First of all, she's supposed to be my friend. Second, she knows how important my reputation is to me. And third, she knows what really happened after the homecoming party. But for some reason, she's been telling people that I spent the night at Ramon's house.

At first, I got really mad when I heard about it. I started thinking about all of the things I could tell on her—true things, too—not like the lie she told about me. I could tell her mom what she hides under the loose board in her closet. I could tell her new boyfriend what she did after the Christmas dance last year. I could tell her brother what really happened to his car.

But I'm not going to. I'll admit part of me really wants to hurt her back, to make her feel what I'm feeling. But when I ask myself what Jesus would do in my situation, that's not the answer I come up with. I'm going to talk to Maria about what she did. I'm going to ask her why she spread the rumor. And then I'm going to tell her exactly how I feel. But I'm not going to be mean about it—and I'm not going to try to get revenge.

It makes sense, when you think about it. If I start saying things about Maria behind her back, she'll get mad and start saying more things about me. Then I'll say more things about her, and the whole thing will keep going in a vicious cycle until we graduate. By doing things God's way, I may be able to save my relationship with Maria. I hope so. I really want to.

Lucia

REAL QUESTION

How are you supposed to react when someone mistreats you?

When someone, especially a close friend, betrays you, it really hurts. There's no question about that. Many people can relate to Lucia. You probably can too.

You've undoubtedly heard the saying, "Don't get mad—get even." It goes hand in hand with "look out for number one." This attitude is seen by many as more attractive than the "turn the other cheek" advice that Christians preach.

Why would telling the truth about Maria to others be hurtful? If you were Lucia, how would you respond to Maria? What would be important to tell Maria about the way you feel? How can a person say what's true about someone and not be hurtful? If you were a friend of Lucia's and saw Maria in the hallway at school, what would you say to her?

REAL answer

Jesus could relate to Maria's feelings. A man whom he handpicked to be his disciple betrayed him for 30 pieces of silver (Matthew 26:2, 14-16), the going price of a slave. And Jesus even washed the feet of his betrayer, Judas Iscariot, the night of his fateful deed!

A couple of years before he was betrayed, Jesus gave some friendship advice during his Sermon on the Mount. Take a look at Matthew 5:38-42. A real friend doesn't take revenge when another friend does something hurtful. A real friend instead "turns the other cheek" when offended. "Turning the other cheek" means giving up your right to take revenge. It means showing kindness and forgiveness to someone who doesn't deserve it. It also means not holding a grudge against the person who hurt you. The apostle Paul outlines a better plan in Romans 12:17-21. Check it out. Contrary to popular belief, it *doesn't* mean being a doormat while someone walks all over you.

Jesus' words aren't easy to swallow! But he practiced what he preached. Instead of getting back at the guy who betrayed him, he went

to the cross to die for the sins of his betrayer and a host of others.
Revenge was never a word in his vocabulary. Is it in yours?

REAL YOU

When I think about how
I've been tempted to take
revenge, I automatically think
about this incident:

_____

_____

_____

_____

_____

_____

_____

_____

_____

_____

_____

_____

_____

_____

_____

_____

_____

_____

Because I want to follow Jesus' example, I need to come clean about any
grudges I have, starting with . . .

_____

_____

_____

_____

_____

_____

_____

_____

_____

_____

_____

_____

_____

_____

_____

_____

_____

_____

_____

_____

_____

_____

_____

_____

_____

Xalted

Witness and Leader

As the son of David, Jesus followed in
his ancestor's footsteps by proclaiming
God's kingdom and being an example of right
behavior. That's why he was given the title
"Witness and leader" (Revelation 1:5). When you give
a godly response to a hurtful action, you are a witness of
God's power to the people around you. When you follow through
on your words with correct behaviors repeatedly, you are leading others by your example.

DAY 4

I find the Jesus Experience when I measure my worth by God's standards.

"What is the price of five sparrows? A couple of pennies? Yet God does not forget a single one of them. And the very hairs on your head are all numbered. So don't be afraid; you are more valuable to him than a whole flock of sparrows."

Luke 12:6-7

REAL XPRESSIONS

True Worth

Sometimes Clarence makes me feel miserable. But I just can't let go of him. Mom and Jackeé both say I should move on. That's easier said than done.

See, I went out of town two weeks ago. When I came back, Jackeé told me that Clarence, my boyfriend of three months, two weeks, and eleven days, had gone out with some girl on Saturday night. I was only gone three days! Jackeé found out through Pam, who happens to be friends with this other girl. At first, I was hoping it was just a rumor.

Clarence didn't even bother to deny it. All he said was, "It didn't mean anything to me." I think he was expecting me to say, "Oh, that's okay." I did that once before. I didn't even know how to respond. I felt so hurt. Clarence just doesn't get it. He can't understand why I'm so upset.

I know I should tell Clarence that it's over. But he's so fun and he's *definitely* fine. I love the fact that out of all the girls, he chose *me.* I feel really special when I'm with him. But I kind of always suspected that he wouldn't be faithful. Too many girls are after him.

Jackeé has been talking about another shaky relationship. She says Delilah ruined Samson's life. (I guess she learned that in church.) She thinks that's what Clarence is doing to me. I know she's right. It's so hard to say no to him, though.

Jackeé said something I'll never forget: "Share, Clarence doesn't treat you right. You're worth more than that to God." Now I just have to live like it.

Sharon

REAL QUESTION

How much are you worth
to Jesus?

Ever think about that? Many people measure their worth by the people
around them. If a couple of people are telling
them, "Hey, you're cool," then they believe they're
OK. All is right with the world. But most times, the
acceptance of others is conditional. It depends on what you
do to earn it.

Is Jesus' acceptance conditional? Some might say yes. Many times,
people doubt their worth to Jesus. This doubt crops up when Jesus fails
to answer their prayers the way that they might want him to or when they
do something they're ashamed of and think Jesus couldn't possibly still
love them. Have you ever felt that way?

Put yourself in Sharon's place. How much is a friendship with the
most popular person you know worth? What would you do to keep a
friendship like this? Would you base your worth on that person's
approval? Why or why not?

REAL ANSWER

Ever count the hairs on
your head? Ever count all
your split ends? God has. No, that's
not what he does for recreation. And he's
not just bored. He just knows the answers to
trivia questions like that and more for one reason.

He cares.

Take a look at Luke 12:6-7, 32. These are a few sound
bites from Jesus' Sermon on the Mount. To get his listeners to
understand God's love for them, Jesus talked to them about birds and
hair. What do the two have in common? God pays attention to both. He
even notices the sparrows—a bird that wasn't worth a high price during
New Testament times. He knows how many hairs you have on your head.
Your own mother doesn't know that info!

God considers you part of his "flock" (12:32). That means he'll do his
best to watch out for you, like a shepherd looks out for the interests of his

sheep. Your worth is also measured by the fact that the Son of God gave up the splendor of heaven to come to earth to die for you (Philippians 2:6-8).

He may not send cards or heart-shaped boxes of chocolates on Valentine's Day or Sweetest Day. But he did something better. He sent the Holy Spirit to live within you 24/7.

You must be pretty special for the Master of the universe to come and hang out with you. Hold on to that thought the next time someone tells you that you're worthless!

real you

I tend to measure my worth by the following yardstick (circle all that apply):

- Friends' approval
- External stuff like looks, grades, etc.
- Other:

_____

_____

_____

_____

_____

_____

_____

_____

_____

_____

_____

_____

_____

_____

_____

_____

_____

_____

_____

I would sum up my understanding of my worth in Jesus this way:

_____

_____

_____

_____

_____

_____

_____

_____

_____

_____

_____

_____

_____

_____

_____

_____

_____

_____

_____

Xalted

Sacrifice

In Old Testament times, the people of Israel had to offer animal sacrifices in order to receive forgiveness for their sins. The animals used were the best the Israelites had. But Jesus' death ended the need for animal sacrifices. He was simply the best God had to offer (Hebrews 9:13-14, 28). His sacrifice shows your immeasurable worth to God. God loves you so much that he gave his very best. And, that's why he desires your best.

DAY 5

I find the Jesus Experience when I accept my place in God's forever family.

But to all who believed him and accepted him, he gave the right to become children of God. They are reborn! This is not a physical birth resulting from human passion or plan—this rebirth comes from God.

John 1:12-13

REAL Xpressions

The Bombshell

I thought I was going to get yelled at for something. That's usually what happens when Dad says, "We need to talk." But when I got to the kitchen, I knew something weird was up. Mom was sitting at the table with a folder in front of her. And she looked nervous.

Before they said anything, they both gave me a big hug. That's when I started to get nervous. I don't remember much of what they said after that. I know Dad said something about me being an answer to their prayers. And I think Mom said something like, "We knew our family wouldn't have been complete without you."

But I wasn't listening. I was too busy staring at the adoption records in the folder on the table. *My* adoption records.

Part of me wants to be mad at them for not telling me sooner that I'm adopted. But another part of me is kind of glad that they kept it a secret. It's bad enough having to deal with something like this in high school. I can't imagine trying to deal with it as a little kid.

My mom and dad—or maybe I should call them my adoptive mom and dad—keep saying, "This doesn't change anything about our family." But they're wrong. It changes everything. My brother is their real son, and my sister is their real daughter. The way I see it, that makes me an outsider.

After I found out, I didn't want to talk to anyone for the longest time—not my friends, not my family, not even Jesus. But then I realized that Jesus probably understands what I'm feeling. After all, Joseph wasn't his real father.

So I started praying. I still feel confused and angry—but at least I have someone to talk to about it.

Michael

REAL QUESTION

When you have trouble
with your family, whose side
is Jesus on?

Having a family can be great. After all,
you can't have a snowball or pillow fight by yourself! And you definitely need someone to yell at for
borrowing your stuff without asking. But sometimes,
living with family can seem like an episode of the game show
"Family Feud" or "So Weird." Other times, it can feel like you're
living in the pages of S. E. Hinton's book, *The Outsider*.

Think about Jesus' family background. How do you think he handled
being an "outsider"? What do you think he'd say to Michael about his
(Michael's) family situation?

REAL ANSWER

Jesus probably
felt like an outsider to
his family. He had a mother,
but no earthly father. His mother
didn't always understand him. (See Luke
2:48.) His brothers (and sisters probably) didn't
get where he was coming from until he died and was
resurrected. Then the light bulb came on.

At one point, they were even embarrassed to call him brother (see John 7:1-5). Imagine having an older brother who thought he was
the Messiah—the Son of God. They didn't fully believe in him, even
though he performed miracles that amazed the crowds. They thought it
was their job to look after him (Mark 3:31-32). They probably wondered
about his sanity at times.

When his family came looking for him once, Jesus had a surprising
thing to say to a crowd of listeners about his family: "Anyone who does
God's will is my brother and sister and mother" (Mark 3:35; see also
Matthew 12:50). Was he dissing his family? Not at all. He was making a
point about his bigger family that he was the head of. Because of Jesus,
anyone who believes in him can belong to the family of God. That's an
eternal family. (See John 1:12.)

Your family might make you feel weird sometimes. You might not feel like you can talk to anyone, because of what's going on. But Jesus understands. When you experience troubles on the *earthly* home front, remember, you can take your troubles to your *heavenly* home. He's been there and he understands!

REAL YOU

This is how I feel most of the time about my family:

_____

_____

_____

_____

_____

_____

_____

_____

_____

_____

_____

_____

_____

_____

_____

_____

_____

The next time I feel like an "outsider," these are some action steps I can take:

_____

_____

_____

_____

_____

_____

_____

_____

_____

_____

_____

_____

_____

_____

_____

_____

XALTED

Wonderful Counselor, Mighty God, Everlasting Father, Prince of Peace

This description of Jesus is recorded in Isaiah 9:6. This is more than just a long title to be read off by an official messenger or announcer. This is like a campaign promise. In Jesus you receive a wonderful counsel from a mighty God, who happens to be an Everlasting Father, and a Prince of Peace. Trusting in him gives you an entry into an eternal family where you'll never feel like an outsider. Because of Jesus, you've been adopted forever into God's family (Galatians 4:5-7).

I find the Jesus Experience when I trust him to help me do what's right in my relationships.

"I have loved you even as the Father has loved me. Remain in my love. When you obey me, you remain in my love, just as I obey my Father and remain in his love."

John 15:9-10

REAL Xpressions

Left Out

OK. I'm jealous. I admit it.

See, Colleen and I had been best friends since third grade—ever since she moved in across the street from me. We did everything together and even liked the same things. We met Sarah in sixth grade when she started going to our middle school. That's when we became "The Trio." Everybody called us that. We're all sophomores now and go to the same high school.

Lately "The Trio" has been "The Duo." Colleen and Sarah began hanging out together more when they started going to the same church this past summer. I belong to a church too—just not theirs. One day, I called Colleen to see about going to a movie on Friday (I was going to call Sarah next) and found out from her mom that she and Sarah had gone to the movie with the youth group at their church!

I called them both up and left a message: "Thanks for not inviting me." I probably shouldn't have done that. But I was hurt. They both apologized when they got home. Everything was cool at first. But then they did the same thing a month later. I found out by accident that their church youth group went skiing. They hadn't even asked me to go. Colleen's excuse was that she knew I had something else to do that weekend. (My grandmother came to visit.) But did that excuse her from at least asking if I could go? Sarah didn't even try to explain it.

After that I thought, *OK. Later for you too!* I stopped inviting them places. Sarah called and asked if I was mad at her for some reason. I told her I didn't have time to talk.

I thought of a million ways to get back at them. But none of my ideas made me feel any better. Well, none of those ideas anyway. I finally had a good idea: I talked to Ginny. Ginny helps out with the youth group at church. She reminded me about Saul in the Bible. Saul was jealous, because God wanted to make David king. Saul's jealousy led him to do some pretty awful things. Then she told me that God cared. I said that I knew that. It's just that right now it's hard for me because I feel left out. My two best friends act like they have more in common with each other than with me.

Cari

REAL QUESTION

A little kid who was afraid of the dark was once told by his parents that Jesus would protect him. But the child replied that he would rather have someone nearby "with skin on." If we're honest, we would say the same thing about our friendships. It's great to know that God cares. But sometimes we want someone nearby "with skin on."

Everyone wants close friends. You're no exception to that, right? That's why when we have them, we want to hang on to them. And when a friend seems to pull away, that can hurt. It leaves the door open to feelings of jealousy and bitterness.

What advice do you have for Cari about Colleen and Sarah? If you could talk to all three of them at the same time, what would you say?

REAL ANSWER

Jealousy comes from the fear that someone is taking away the love or friendship of someone special to you. You've probably heard at least one story showing the dark side of jealousy. That's why it's described this way in Proverbs 27:4: "Anger is cruel, and wrath is like a flood, but who can survive the destructiveness of jealousy?" Jealousy often leads to other problems. Remember Cain and Abel? Jealousy is also listed in the middle of some pretty nasty sins in Galatians 5:19-21.

Jealousy can also come from a feeling of ownership. We want to keep what "belongs" to us. The funny thing about people is that we can't own any of them. Most friendships don't come with a guarantee that they'll last forever. Many of them end after you change schools or neighborhoods. Some might even end after you change your deodorant (or choose not to wear one).

There's only one relationship that is guaranteed to last forever: the one you have with Jesus. (Saw that one coming, didn't you?) Need a written guarantee? Here it is: "Remain in me, and I will remain in you" (John 15:4). Here's another news flash: "You didn't choose me. I chose you" (John 15:16). You were chosen by the God of the universe to have a unique relationship that blows away all earthly relationships. As a sign of his remaining in you, he sent the Holy Spirit to take up space within you. The Holy Spirit helps you to react in godly ways. That's why Jesus also said, "You are my friends if you obey me" (John 15:14). Your friendship with Jesus really soars when you are walking in obedience.

Being secure in Jesus' love is the cure for jealousy.

Real you

Jesus, I am so glad to have you as my friend. Here's what I think is great about our relationship:

_____

_____

_____

_____

_____

_____

_____

_____

_____

_____

_____

_____

To get more out of my relationship with Jesus, I need to take the following steps:

_____

_____

_____

_____

_____

_____

_____

_____

_____

_____

_____

_____

_____

_____

XALTED

Bread of Life

What food item couldn't you live without? Pizza? Steak? Ice cream? Chips? How about bread? Bread satisfies hunger more than . . . well, chips. A relationship with Jesus is the same way. That's why Jesus calls himself the "bread of life" (John 6:48). Many of the poorest people in New Testament times only had bread to eat. They understood that bread was necessary for survival. Jesus wants you to realize that he's necessary for your survival too. He wants you to feed on him daily.

I find the Jesus Experience when I make good choices in my relationships.

"I have come as a light to shine in this dark world, so that all who put their trust in me will no longer remain in the darkness."

John 12:46

REAL Xpressions

The Right Team

One major decision down, another to go.

I was at a Young Life meeting this summer, just hanging out with some friends while my girlfriend and her family were in Europe. (They always go there for the summer.) I wasn't interested in God or anything like that. One of my friends just said it would be a good time, so I said I'd go.

The guy in charge got up and started talking about how he used to feel empty inside and how he tried to hide it by partying all the time. That sounded familiar to me. Then he talked about how he found God and how his life changed forever.

I ran into the guy later, and we started talking about things that were going on in my life. One thing led to another, and I ended up praying with him and giving my life to Christ.

That was Major Decision #1, and it turned out to be awesome. I'm in a great Bible study now, and I'm learning things about being a Christian that I never knew before.

Now comes Major Decision #2. One of the things we've been talking about in Bible study is surrounding yourself with people who will encourage you in your walk with Christ. That's definitely not my girlfriend. She's not into anything spiritual at all. (She'll probably laugh when I tell her what happened to me.)

I still love her, but I realize that I can't stay in a relationship with her. When she gets back from Europe, I'm going to ask her if we can be just friends for a while. Then I'm going to tell her the same thing that guy at the Young Life meeting told me. If she likes what she hears, maybe there's hope for our relationship. If not, I'll keep talking to her—as a friend—for as long as she'll listen.

Dan

REAL QUESTION

Does being a follower of
Jesus mean that you can't
have friends who aren't Christians?

Have you ever heard people talk
about Christians as "exclusive"? In other
words, Christians should only hang around with
other Christians. What's your take on that?

If you're a Christian, think back to the time when you
first believed. Who influenced you to believe in Jesus? How did
your life change as a result? Maybe, like Dan, you began reconsider-
ing some of your friendships and relationships.

Think about Dan's Major Decision #2. Would you consider it right for
Dan to break up with his girlfriend simply because she doesn't believe
the way that he does? What would you do?

REAL ANSWER

Let's face it: all of Jesus'
friends were non-Christians
at one point. Jesus had a rep as
someone who hung around with sinners
(Matthew 9:9-11; Luke 15:1-2). His whole reason
for doing that is because he came "to seek and to
save those . . . who are lost" (Luke 19:10). As the "light of
the world" (John 8:12), Jesus came to bring hope to people
stuck in the darkness of sin. That includes us.

Some relationships, however, tempt you over to the dark side, rather
than point you to the light. For example, a former drug user might be
tempted back into drug use if she continues to hang out with her drug
buddies. Or if you had a friend who continually encouraged you to
shoplift or cheat on tests, you might want to reevaluate that relationship.

Years after Jesus' resurrection, the apostle Paul cautioned: "Don't team
up with those who are unbelievers. . . . How can light live with darkness?"
(2 Corinthians 6:14). That's why believers are warned not to marry unbelievers. For long-term relationships, people need to be going in the same
direction, rather than working against one another. Dating non-Christians
can be a very slippery slope. If someone's values are not the same as yours,
you have to ask yourself why you want to date this particular person.

But that doesn't mean that believers can never associate with those who aren't Christians. You might be the only "light" your friends see.

God wants you to honor him through your relationships. The best way to do that is to communicate with him about your relationships. Ask him to guide you (and protect you) in your relationships.

ReaL You

One way I can be "light" to
my non-believing friends is to:

_____

_____

_____

_____

_____

_____

_____

_____

_____

_____

_____

_____

_____

_____

_____

_____

_____

_____

_____

I show that Jesus has first place in my life by the following actions:

_____

_____

_____

_____

_____

_____

_____

_____

_____

_____

_____

_____

_____

_____

_____

_____

_____

_____

_____

_____

_____

_____

_____

_____

_____

_____

_____

_____

Xalted

Word of Life

You probably have heard the expression, "What's the good word?" Essentially, it means "Tell me something good." In the Bible, Jesus is not only known as the "Word," he's also known as the "Word of Life" (Philippians 2:16). So, what does that mean? Good question. It means that he's God *and* good news in the flesh. The good news is that he offers you eternal life—life that lasts forever. And you can count on him to keep his word.

DAY 8

I find the Jesus Experience when I share the hope I find in Jesus with others who are hurting.

"I am leaving you with a gift—peace of mind and heart. And the peace I give isn't like the peace the world gives. So don't be troubled or afraid."

John 14:27

REAL Xpressions

A Rock and a Hard Place

Can you believe I laughed when my sister told me she tried to kill herself? I didn't think she was serious. I mean, I know she's been depressed lately. But suicide? No way. But when she showed me the empty bottle of sleeping pills, I realized she was serious, and I just lost it.

She said, "You're the only person who knows about this. If you tell anyone, I'll never be able to trust you again."

Nothing like putting a little pressure on someone! If I'm the only person who knows, that means I'm the only one who can stop her from trying again. All of a sudden I felt like I had to say the "right" thing to her, like I had to give her a reason to keep living.

I tried to tell her about Jonah—you know, the whale guy in the Bible—and how depressed he got when things went bad in his life. I tried to tell her that God didn't desert Jonah, no matter how depressed he got. I was hoping that might mean something to her. I don't think it did. I'm not even sure she heard me.

I'm going to keep talking to her, that's for sure. I'm going to keep telling her that God loves her and that I love her. And I'm going to tell someone else about our secret—someone who can help her more than I can. Someone with professional experience. She may get mad at me, but I can live with that. Right now I'm more concerned with keeping her alive than worrying that she might get mad at me.

If I can help her get through whatever's going on in her life right now, we'll have the rest of our lives to rebuild our trust relationship.

Liz

REAL QUESTION

Some situations in life are beyond "pat" answers. Depression is one of them. Depressed people aren't sure what's good about life. Many feel they don't have much to live for. They may not even know why they're depressed.

Depression isn't the problem. It is the symptom of a problem. Sometimes, an ongoing illness, broken relationships, financial worries, or some other issue lies beneath the surface. Fear is usually at the bottom of depression.

What would you say to Liz's sister? What do you think she needs more than anything? Have you known someone like Liz's sister who thought about suicide? Is saying, "I'll pray for you" really enough?

REAL ANSWER

Jesus knew that he was going to die soon. So, at the last meal he shared with his followers before his death, he wanted to make a few things clear to them. You can read his words in John 14. He told them not to be afraid. He also told them that he was going away to prepare a place for them. Why would he tell them that? Because he knew that life would be even harder for them after he left. For one thing, they were about to lose the leader they loved. Jesus was headed to the cross to die. For another, the persecution they would soon face was enough to depress or make anyone fearful. But the most important reason for telling them that was because he loved them.

That's why Jesus also told them that he would send the Holy Spirit to be with them (14:26). He followed that up with the promise of peace (14:27). Then, in chapter 16, he ended with this: "I have told you all this so that you may have peace in me. Here on earth you will have many trials and sorrows. But take heart, because I have overcome the world" (16:33).

A depressed person needs hope, rather than pat answers. That's what Jesus offered his disciples hours before he was arrested and crucified. Sometimes when life doesn't make sense, we have to hold on to the promise that he will give us peace in those times (Philippians 4:7). He promises us in Isaiah 26:3, "You will keep in perfect peace all who trust in you, whose thoughts are fixed on you!" Turning our thoughts from focusing on our problems to focusing on God is the key—and that can take some time. A depressed person needs time to heal. Most of all, a depressed person needs God. And he needs to know that God's purpose for his life is not over yet!

real you

This is what I can say to someone I know who is depressed or going through a tough time:

_____

_____

_____

_____

_____

_____

_____

_____

_____

_____

_____

_____

_____

_____

_____

_____

_____

_____

_____

When I think about facing tough times, I will remember these three truths about Jesus:

_____

_____

_____

_____

_____

_____

_____

_____

_____

_____

_____

_____

_____

_____

_____

_____

_____

_____

_____

_____

_____

_____

_____

Xalted

Way

You might have heard people from
other religions talk about the different
"paths" they've followed to God. During the
Last Supper, Jesus reminded his followers that he
was the only way to God (John 14:6). There were no
ifs, ands, or buts about it. He is the only way to God.
Period. And, in tough times, he is the "way" out!

DAY 9

I find the Jesus Experience when I trust in God's plan for sex.

"But God's plan was seen from the beginning of creation, for 'He made them male and female.' 'This explains why a man leaves his father and mother and is joined to his wife, and the two are united into one.' Since they are no longer two but one, let no one separate them, for God has joined them together."

Mark 10:6-9

REAL XPRESSIONS

White Wedding

My friends think the reason I'm still a virgin is that I want to be able to wear white on my wedding day. Can you believe that? Like I have some kind of superstition about the color of my wedding gown. I told them that if that were true, I would have had sex a long time ago. Hey, if sex were as good as everybody says it is, I'd have tried it even if it meant I had to wear a plaid wedding dress.

What I'm doing *is* waiting for something better than "good." I'm waiting for something perfect. I know that God's plan for the ultimate loving relationship—a husband and wife giving themselves totally to each other—beats anything my friends talk about. And I'm willing to wait as long as necessary to make sure that I get that kind of relationship.

Some of my friends say they sleep with their boyfriends because they "love" them. But when I hear guys talk about it, it's like love is the last thing on their mind. And what happens when they break up? (Which they *always* do.) It's like the sex between them loses all of its meaning.

I don't want that to happen with me. I don't want to ever have to worry about whether the guy I give my virginity to loves me or not. I want to know that we can enjoy sex with each other for the rest of our lives. That's why I'm going to do things according to God's timetable.

Kelsey

REAL QUESTION

Did Jesus say that sex before marriage is wrong?

Think about the shows or movies you've seen recently. According to society, what are the ingredients that make a good dating relationship? Are these on your list?

For many people, sex is an automatic ingredient of a relationship. Many people believe that sex just naturally follows "love" and don't believe that they need to put any limits on how they express that love with their significant other.

So, why is wearing a white wedding gown so important to Kelsey? Is this important to you? Would you want this to be important to your future spouse and your future kids?

REAL ANSWER

Sex is one of the most talked about subjects around. There's nothing wrong with sex. After all, God invented it. But with God, there is a purpose for everything.

As recorded in the Gospel of Mark, Jesus quoted from Genesis 1:27 and 2:24 to remind his listeners of God's design for marriage. Two people would become one. This isn't a magician's trick. It shows the level of intimacy two people share. Sex is the physical expression of that intimacy. It is not meant to be cheapened by the experimentation of two people who aren't even sure they like each other. It is also not a bargaining chip to be used to hold on to a relationship.

Paul, one of Jesus' followers and the author of most of the New Testament, knew God's plan for marriage. That's why he could strongly urge the readers of First Corinthians to "run away from sexual sin" (1 Corinthians 6:18). He brought this up about five times in this letter and in other letters. (See Romans 13:13; 1 Corinthians 6:13; 10:8.) In 1 Thessalonians 4:3-5, Paul tells us to be different from the world. Does this mean that sex is wrong? No way. But sex outside of God's plan is. God created you, he created sex, and he knows what's best for you. If you will be patient and wait on God, who has a plan for your life, he will work it out for you. His plan includes all areas of your life, including your romantic life—especially your sex life. God may choose to call you to a life of singleness, so that you can be fully devoted to him (see 1 Corinthians 7:1, 32-35). If he does that, he will give you the peace to accept it.

REAL YOU

This is what I've always believed about sex before or after marriage:

_____

_____

_____

_____

_____

_____

_____

_____

_____

_____

_____

_____

_____

_____

_____

_____

_____

This is what I would tell my friends about God's design for marriage:

_____

_____

_____

_____

_____

_____

_____

_____

_____

_____

_____

_____

_____

_____

_____

_____

_____

_____

_____

_____

_____

_____

_____

Xalted

Mighty Power

Who is the most powerful person you
know? A corporate CEO? The president of the
United States? Your best friend? Paul described
Jesus as a "mighty power" (2 Corinthians 13:3). That
means he can do anything. When you're facing temp-
tation, a corporate CEO can't do much for you except pray
that God will help you. When you need *real* power to handle
tough situations and temptations, remember to go straight to the
Source, Jesus. He will help you overcome (1 Corinthians 10:13).

Ever watch a movie or a TV show where someone talks about the guilt he or she feels? Usually, that person reclines on a couch in a psychiatrist's office and painfully weaves a sad tale of past wrongs. That's why many people see guilt as horrible and undesirable. It's like the sweater your great-aunt got you for Christmas when she forgot how old you were or the fact that you wouldn't be caught dead in something like that.

GUILT AND FORGIVENESS

Guilt is something everyone experiences at some point in life. It nags at you like a loose tooth or a pain that won't go away. Some guilt is human-made—something we slap on each other out of our own weaknesses. Some guilt is from Satan, the enemy of believers—leftovers from past sins that were already dealt with. But some guilt is God-breathed.

In *The Problem of Pain,* C. S. Lewis explained, "God whispers to us in our pleasures, speaks in our conscience, but shouts in our pains: it is His megaphone to rouse a deaf world." Guilt is part of that megaphone message. Guilt itself *isn't* the problem. It's a *symptom* of a problem—more than likely, a *sin problem* that needs to be addressed.

Some people try to handle guilt by ignoring it. "If I don't talk about it, it's not there." Some try to escape from it by partying harder or throwing themselves into good causes. Others at least are willing to talk about the fact that they feel guilty. But these solutions are like taking two aspirin to cure a broken toe. They may deaden the pain for a while. But the problem remains.

Unresolved guilt has an increasing effect. The more you try to ignore it or escape from it, the stronger it can seem. Many people have ended their lives because of guilt. They simply couldn't make the pain go away.

So, how can a person deal with guilt in a healthy way? Stay tuned. You're about to find out.

I find the Jesus Experience when I accept *his* standards and truth, rather than my own.

"And when he comes, he will convince the world of its sin, and of God's righteousness, and of the coming judgment."

John 16:8

REAL χPRESSIONS

Dilemma

Dr. Silbert is known for his quirks. He looks out over the top of his thick glasses and has this strange way of clearing his throat every few seconds. He's really nice and always invites me into his office to talk. He knows everything about economics, but he just can't teach it. His tests are so impossible, and since he's completely oblivious, most students cheat. On test days, cheat sheets float all around. As soon as he hands the test out, he leaves the room for at least 45 minutes. He's very trusting. Way too trusting.

So that's my dilemma. I've never cheated on one of his tests. This is the last test before the final exam, and I *have* to do well in this class. I have to get a 3.0 in order to keep my scholarship. I'll never pass this test on my own. I've been going to study sessions, visiting Dr. Silbert during office hours, and studying for the last two weeks for this test. No matter how much I study, I'll never be able to learn all this by next Wednesday. As much as I like Dr. Silbert, this is ridiculous.

If I could write just a few things down for the test, that would be enough. I've gone over all this stuff. I'll just need some prompts during the exam. I have no choice—I *have* to pass this test. That's understandable, isn't it?

I've been thinking about this for the past two days straight. I just have this nagging feeling of guilt that won't leave me alone. I know that Jesus wouldn't approve if I cheat. Period. There's no way around that one. He hates cheating; he loves honesty. No matter how I try to justify it, he's not budging. He's making me so uncomfortable! I guess that's his strategy.

Jalen

REAL QUESTION

Does Jesus care more
about us following his rules
than he does about us?

Have you ever been caught in a bind
like Jalen's? It's a no-win situation. If he doesn't
cheat, he winds up failing the test. If he does cheat,
he winds up losing in another way.

Situations like these have led some people to question
some of God's commands. Maybe you or someone else you know
has said or thought, *If only God understood what I'm up against! It's
not always easy to obey, especially now!*

The process of trying to find a solution to a tough situation can sometimes lead to guilty feelings. Have you ever experienced that "nagging
feeling of guilt" that Jalen talked about? Have you ever wondered why
God stirs up these feelings? Do you think he just wants to make people
miserable?

If you were Jalen, what would you do? Do you think the end justifies
the means? When caught in a difficult situation, have you ever hoped for
a third option, you know, the easy way out?

REAL answer

Before Jesus left the earth,
he promised his disciples
that he would send the Holy Spirit.
Part of the Holy Spirit's job was and still
is to "convince the world of its sin, and of God's
righteousness" (John 16:8). Jesus promised that the
Holy Spirit would lead believers "into all truth" (John
14:17). Need an instant replay of that? Here it is: He "will
guide you into all truth" (John 16:13). Sometimes the truth he
guides us into is that uncomfortable, nagging feeling that we've done
something wrong and need to own up to it. Yet, this kind of guilt leads
to repentance (see 2 Corinthians 7:9-11). If viewed properly, this kind of
guilt can lead to real change, making you a better person.

When it comes to sin, God doesn't compromise, nor does he make
allowances for compromise. The God who "is the same yesterday, today,

and forever" (Hebrews 13:8), still has the same standards in regard to sin. Rationalizing doesn't cut it with him. Turning away from sin does.

God takes no pleasure in making his children feel guilty. But he uses guilt to bring his people back to him. God doesn't nag forever, though. He knows the human heart. The person who is determined to ignore God's reminders of the truth will someday find himself without them. (See 1 Timothy 4:2.) In other words, they no longer have a conscience for their sin.

Do you want that?

REAL YOU

Here are several times when Jesus used guilt to bring me back to him and how I reacted to his prompting:

_____

_____

_____

_____

_____

_____

_____

_____

_____

_____

_____

_____

_____

_____

_____

_____

_____

_____

_____

_____

_____

_____

_____

When I'm tempted to rationalize my sin, instead of paying attention to that nagging feeling of guilt, I'll try to take these three steps instead:

_____

_____

_____

_____

_____

_____

_____

_____

_____

_____

_____

_____

_____

_____

_____

_____

_____

Xalted

Wisdom

Ever search high and low to find someone? According to Proverbs 8:17, Wisdom is described as someone to search for. Wisdom is not only someone to seek, it is also given. When the world was created, wisdom was there. Jesus has been described as full of wisdom (Luke 2:40; 2:52) and wisdom itself. "For our benefit God made Christ to be wisdom itself" (1 Corinthians 1:30). When guilt crops up, the wise person seeks wisdom.

I find the Jesus Experience when I accept his forgiveness for any sin I've committed.

"We deserve to die for our evil deeds, but this man hasn't done anything wrong." Then he said, "Jesus, remember me when you come into your Kingdom. And Jesus replied, "I assure you, today you will be with me in paradise."

Luke 23:41-43

"With my authority, take this message of repentance to all the nations, beginning in Jerusalem: 'There is forgiveness of sins for all who turn to me.'"

Luke 24:47

REAL Xpressions

The Lost Years

My mom used to have a picture of me that she kept on her piano. I remember it was taken during the summer of my freshman year, on a missions trip to Mexico. In the picture, I'm standing in front of a bunch of Mexican kids, with a Bible in my hand and a big smile on my face. Mom used to say that the picture showed the real me.

I wonder if she still has it.

For all I know, she threw it out, along with everything else of mine, when I left. I wouldn't blame her if she did.

I suppose I could talk about why a good Christian boy started using drugs or how long it takes a person to realize he's an addict or how many times I've been arrested or how long I've been on the streets or what I've had to do to survive. But those things don't matter now.

Last week I was trying to score some money for a hit when this guy offered to take me to lunch. It's usually a bad sign when somebody wants you to go somewhere with him. But I needed to eat, and the guy didn't look like a psycho, so I said okay.

While we were eating, he looked at me and said, "Do you know God loves you?" I didn't say anything to him. I just ate my food and walked out. But then I started thinking about that picture on my mom's piano and what she used to say about the "real me." And I started wondering whether God really could love someone who's done what I've done—someone who's ruined not only his own life, but the lives of everyone who cared about him.

And I thought I heard a little voice in my head say, "I've always loved you."

Eddie

REAL QUESTION

Does Jesus really have the power to forgive us when we blow it—*really* blow it? We've all messed up at some point in our lives. Maybe you know someone like Eddie, who really has gone off course. Maybe you have even been in Eddie's shoes. Maybe you still are.

Many people have a private list of the sins that they think are worse than others. When have you feared that something you've done is the "unforgivable sin" (Matthew 12:31)—the one sin that cannot be forgiven?

Imagine being Eddie in that restaurant. How would you respond to the person beside you? How would you reply to the "little voice" inside? What effect does remembering that picture on the piano have on your response? Is forgiveness too impossible to hope for?

REAL ANSWER

One of Jesus' most well-known parables is the parable of the loving father (Luke 15:11-32). You've probably heard it a million times. But have you really *taken in* the message of the parable? The son had demanded his inheritance early. That was like saying to his father, "I wish you were dead." Then, after blowing it all and nearly starving to death, the son decided to wander back home. He didn't think his father would take him back.

But he did.

That's the story of forgiveness. It's a picture of what God does every day. Jesus was a walking canvas of this. He often ate with "tax collectors and sinners"—people considered to be the scum of the earth in Jewish society. (See Matthew 9:10.) The Pharisees—the religious leaders—often criticized Jesus for doing that. That's why after dining in the home of a tax collector, Jesus announced that he came to "seek and save those like him who are lost" (Luke 19:10). In other words, he offers forgiveness to those who need it. That includes everyone!

Need another snapshot? Picture a gloomy hillside where three people are dying. Two men are paying for the wrong choices they had made. The other one is dying to pay the price for the wrong choices *the other two* had made. One of the other two decides to make a right choice for a change. He turns to the third guy—the only one who can help him now. (See Luke 23:40-43.) Like the prodigal son, he returns home. The third guy—Jesus—forgives him.

That's why Jesus laid this out for his followers: "The thief's purpose is to steal and kill and destroy. My purpose is to give life in all its fullness" (John 10:10). The thief is Satan. His aim is to magnify guilt—to make it seem so big that nothing can ever take it away. But God wants you to believe that *he's* so big that he can deal with even the worst thing that you can do. (See Romans 8:1-2.)

By the way, the one sin that cannot be forgiven is to accuse God of using Satan's power to work miracles. That's what the Pharisees accused Jesus of doing. That puts a whole different perspective on the subject, doesn't it?

REAL YOU

This is what I've always believed about Jesus' forgiveness:

_____

_____

_____

_____

_____

_____

_____

_____

_____

_____

_____

_____

_____

_____

Here are three areas in my life where I need to talk to Jesus about forgiveness:

_____

_____

_____

_____

_____

_____

_____

_____

_____

_____

_____

_____

_____

_____

_____

_____

_____

XALTED

Mighty to Save

Superheroes have power to stop bullets or melt steel with their laser vision. But they're not real. (You knew that was coming.) Zephaniah 3:17 describes the Messiah as "a mighty savior." Jesus is that Messiah. That means he's the only one who has the power to save you from the worst enemy of your life—sin. He is "mighty to save," no matter what you've done. Best of all, his power doesn't depend on whether any kryptonite is available.

I find the Jesus Experience when I forgive like he does.

"If you forgive those who sin against you, your heavenly Father will forgive you. But if you refuse to forgive others, your Father will not forgive your sins."

Matthew 6:14-15

REAL Xpressions

The Family "Problem"

My dad calls it his "elbow problem." (He says he bends his elbow too often when he has a drink in his hand. Ha ha.) My mom calls it "the family legacy." Dad's parents were both alcoholics, and so are his two brothers.

Dad never uses the "A-word" (as he calls it), but he knows he has a problem. I think that's why he started going to church with us in the first place. He figured if he could get God to help him, everything would be OK.

When he gave his life to Christ a few months later, I figured he was right. He told Mom that since he was "born again," he was going to live his new life right—and that meant no more drinking.

He didn't go to rehab or Alcoholics Anonymous or anything like that. He just stopped—cold turkey. Mom sent my sister and me to stay with our cousins in Indiana for a couple weeks, and when we came home Dad wasn't drinking anymore.

Life was great for about a year or so after that. Dad got a big promotion at work and even volunteered to teach Sunday school. Then things started to change—not all at once, but a little at a time. We noticed some of Dad's old habits creeping back into his life—coming home late, calling in sick to work, and trying to hide beer in the old refrigerator in the garage.

When I think about him drinking again, I just get sick. Part of me just wants to give up on him and say, "He's never going to change." But I don't think that's what God wants me to do.

Ron

REAL QUESTION

Does Jesus expect us to forgive someone who continually wrongs us?

Some of the hurts in life are difficult to forgive. Living with a parent or sibling who disappoints or continually lies can be unbearable. Maybe that's why many people believe that forgiveness comes with a "three strikes and you're out" policy. You offer it three times to the same person for the same offense and you're done. Some people also believe that God has a limit on how much he forgives. What do you think?

If you were a friend of Ron's what would you say to him? Now put yourself in Ron's place. You're face-to-face with your dad. What would you say to him? Is there a limit to the amount of forgiveness you can offer?

REAL answer

The apostle Peter once asked Jesus a question about forgiveness (Matthew 18:21). Peter asked, "How often should I forgive someone who sins against me? Seven times?" Even the rabbis of that day only required three times to forgive someone. Jesus' answer was much higher than that! The number (seventy times seven) wasn't meant to be followed exactly. ("Let's see, I've forgiven you 76 times. After the next one, it's over for you, dude!") It was his way of saying, "Keep on forgiving." In other words, there are no limits on forgiveness.

The point is that God expects his people to forgive one another. Check out Matthew 18:35 and the Lord's Prayer (Matthew 6:14-15). Colossians 3:13 urges us, "You must make allowance for each other's faults and forgive the person who offends you. Remember the Lord forgave you, so you must forgive others." We must forgive in order to be forgiven. Does that make forgiveness automatic? Not always. Sometimes we can't forgive without God's help.

Forgiving a person doesn't mean that the person in the wrong has no responsibility in the matter. The Bible also is clear on what a person needs to do when someone has sinned against him. Matthew 18:15-17 explains the process. You do the math. Let's say that Person B wronged Person A. Person A has an obligation to confront Person B. If Person B refuses to acknowledge his wrong, Person A can then bring another person to confront Person B again. If Person B still doesn't listen, those two persons are to go tell a pastor or a church leader.

Forgiveness doesn't mean that the person who wrongs you will never wrong you again. Life has no guarantees. Offering forgiveness just means that you're doing what God asks you to do.

ReaL you

As I think about Jesus' command to forgive, I will mentally erase the limit I've set in my mind for forgiveness. (One time? Two times? Three times?) Some of the things that have held me back from forgiving someone else are . . .

_____

_____

_____

_____

_____

_____

_____

_____

_____

_____

_____

_____

_____

_____

_____

_____

_____

_____

I'm having a hard time forgiving _____ . I need to either offer forgiveness to this person or ask God to help me forgive. Lord, today, I ask . . .

_____

_____

_____

_____

_____

_____

_____

_____

_____

_____

_____

_____

_____

_____

_____

_____

Xalted

Prince of Peace

If you've heard Handel's *Messiah,* you
know that Jesus is called the Prince of
Peace. That's a title taken from Isaiah 9:6.
When you think of peace, what comes to mind?
Many people think about war, which is the opposite
of peace. Sin creates war between two individuals. Jesus'
death makes peace with God possible. Forgiveness is like a peace
treaty between two warring camps. With whom do you need to forge a
peace treaty? What's stopping you? Ask the Prince of Peace to mediate.

I find the Jesus Experience when I let go of attitudes that hold me back.

"The thorny ground represents those who hear and accept the Good News, but all too quickly the message is crowded out by the cares of this life, the lure of wealth, and the desire for nice things, so no crop is produced."

Mark 4:18-19

REAL XPRESSIONS

Me, Jealous?

Hey, I'm not bitter. Why should I be? Just because my roommate's dad bought him a Jeep Grand Cherokee as a graduation gift? Just because my parents can't afford to give me even a used set of wheels for graduation? Me, bitter? No way! Well . . . maybe I was for a while.

Zach has been given his life on a silver platter. His parents just throw money at him. They've got plenty to throw, too. When I mentioned Zach's gift to my parents (hoping they'd get the hint), they just laughed. Later, my dad bought me a toy car as a joke. Ha ha. Good one, Dad!

Zach took me for a ride in the Jeep. It was sweet. He kept pointing out its features. I had to swallow the sarcasm that kept threatening to come up. I laughed when he hit a pothole! I told him, "Hey, you might've broken an axle or something."

I felt crummy after that. I knew I had a serious attitude problem about that car. So, I went and talked with my friend, Bob. He was like a mentor to me my freshman year. All the guys would go to him with problems. He lives in my apartment building. After I told him about Zach, he said, "Sounds like a case of envy, man, plain and simple." I wanted to deny it, but I couldn't. Then he told me, "Nick, don't be like Ahab."

He had to fill me in on that one. I'm a Christian and all, but I didn't know much about Ahab. He showed me the story. See, this dude Ahab wanted a vineyard that belonged to someone else. He was willing to do whatever it took to get it. I got chills just reading it.

I never thought of myself as someone who is greedy about anything. But this time, there was no denying it. I prayed and asked God to forgive me.

Nick

REAL QUESTION

Can we really trust that Jesus is there for us when life seems unfair?

Ever want something you couldn't have? Knowing that someone has what you want can really stink. In 1 Kings 21, Ahab really wanted a vineyard owned by a guy named Naboth. According to the law of the Israelites, Naboth had the right to say no to Ahab's offer to buy his vineyard. But Ahab couldn't take no for an answer and took what he wanted. When the prophet Elijah brought the matter to his attention, Ahab didn't seek God's forgiveness for his actions. Instead, he lashed out in bitterness.

Nick could relate to those feelings. How does Nick's attitude change from the beginning of the story to the end? What caused the change? How do you think his conversation with Zach would have changed if Jesus had actually been there with him in the car?

Put yourself in Nick's place. When have you felt like that? How did you deal with your feelings?

REAL ANSWER

More than likely, our reaction when we complain that life is unfair comes from how much we trust God. In the parable of the seeds (Mark 4:3-20), Jesus described the seed that fell on thorny ground. It took root, but the thorns and weeds quickly choked the tender blades so that nothing came of it. Remember what Jesus said were the thorns? He said, "the cares of this life, *the lure of wealth, and the desire for nice things.*" Got that? The desire to have more and more stuff, if left unchecked, can snuff out a relationship with God. It can lead to lack of trust, bitterness, envy, jealousy—all the feelings that Nick experienced.

A lack of trust in God can sometimes lead to sin. Once Nick admitted the root of the problem—envy—he realized that he needed God's forgiveness. We all do. Everyone, every day, sins. It's part of our human nature ever since Adam and Eve disobeyed God. Built into the Lord's Prayer is a plea for forgiveness. Check out Luke 11:4 (also Matthew 6:12). Jesus knew that we'd blow it occasionally. Guilt is usually the early warning sign that something is wrong.

Does knowing that God forgives us mean we have the right to go out and sin as much as we want to? Not at all. God wants his people to walk with integrity. When we fail to do that, our credibility as his witnesses is damaged. You probably know someone who talks a good game as a Christian, but whose actions fall short of godly living.

Yeah, we've all blown it. But God offers us grace. You know what grace is. It's not just a pre-dinner thank you. It's something undeserved. That's why the Bible says "if we confess our sins to him, he is faithful and just to forgive us and to cleanse us from every wrong" (1 John 1:9). We don't deserve God's forgiveness. But he gives it to us anyway.

REAL YOU

This is one time that I know Jesus would say that I needed a serious attitude check:

_____

_____

_____

_____

_____

_____

_____

_____

_____

_____

_____

_____

_____

_____

_____

_____

_____

_____

_____

_____

_____

This is what I appreciate most about the forgiveness Jesus offers:

_____

_____

_____

_____

_____

_____

_____

_____

_____

_____

_____

_____

_____

_____

_____

_____

Xalted

Sun of Righteousness

The Son, like the sun, came to shed light on a dark place. Jesus makes it possible for anyone who trusts him to be right with God. Jesus' righteousness makes up for our lack of righteousness. It also sheds light on our dark attitudes and reminds us that we need his forgiveness. To those who desire to obey him, "The Sun of Righteousness will rise with healing in his wings" (Malachi 4:2).

I find the Jesus Experience when I accept the fact that all of us need forgiveness.

"How terrible it will be for you teachers of religious law and you Pharisees. Hypocrites! You are so careful to clean the outside of the cup and the dish, but inside you are filthy—full of greed and self-indulgence! Blind Pharisees! First wash the inside of the cup, and then the outside will become clean, too."

Matthew 23:25-26

REAL Xpressions

A Good Person

My life's not like one of those Hallmark TV specials. You know the kind where the druggie son or daughter comes back home after dissing Mom and Pop. No. I was always the dutiful daughter. Never gave my mom (my dad's dead) any trouble. Got good grades in school—good enough to finish high school this summer early. I even went to church on Sundays.

Still, for the first time in 17 years (I'm 17) I had this feeling that something was wrong.

I don't know when the feeling started actually. . . . OK. Maybe I do. An evangelist came to speak at our church a month ago on Youth Sunday. He started talking about sin and stuff. I'd heard all that before. I was raised in church. I knew he wasn't really talking to me. I had a list in my head of some of the kids in youth church he might have been talking about.

It was when he said, "I'll bet you think you're a good person" that I started paying attention. He brought up the story Jesus told about the prodigal son. But he skipped all the stuff about the prodigal leaving and started talking about the brother who stayed behind. Maybe he hadn't run wild like his brother. But the fact that he refused to celebrate when his brother returned home meant something.

Then the speaker asked us if good people sinned. And that's when I knew what that feeling was I'd been having. Guilt.

You see, I didn't think I'd done anything that needed God's forgiveness. I kept thinking that sin was stuff like murder, telling lies, selling pornography, etc. I thought I was the one exception to the "all have sinned" rule. I had to ask God to forgive me for thinking that I was too good to need his forgiveness.

Emily

REAL QUESTION

Is anyone "good" in Jesus' eyes? Is being "good enough" good enough?

Most people, if they're honest, probably consider themselves to be good. Like Emily, they may have been raised in a church environment or haven't rebelled in a major way. Maybe they're even kind to children and animals.

Know anyone like that? Are you like that? If you could have a conversation with Emily, what would you tell her? Why would that be important? If Emily met Jesus face-to-face, what do you think he would tell her about herself? Why?

REAL ANSWER

Jesus had several run-ins with "good" people. Mark 10:17-22 has the scoop on one encounter. This guy thought he had it all. Ever since he was a child, he had obeyed the Ten Commandments, or at least the ones Jesus named. But Jesus knew that one thing kept this man from fully giving his life to Jesus. His possessions were too important to him.

Being good just wasn't good enough.

Jesus constantly clashed with the Pharisees, another group of "good" religious people. Check out Jesus' tough words to them in Matthew 23. The Pharisees claimed that they kept all the rules and regulations of the Law. They even made up their own rules. They did everything right. But one thing they lacked—the ability to admit that they needed God's forgiveness for the wrongs they committed. Jesus told them that they would die with their sins unforgiven.

Being good just wasn't good enough.

God has this to say to all "good people": "All have sinned; all fall short of God's glorious standard" (Romans 3:23). But there is good news: "Yet now God in his gracious kindness declares us not guilty. He has done this through Christ Jesus, who has freed us by taking away our sins" (Romans 3:24). He took all our wrongdoings on himself on the cross and gave us his goodness.

As part of God's creation, we're "good." That just means that God's work in creating us is good. But as Jesus told the rich young ruler, "Only God is truly good" (Mark 10:18). That's why we need his forgiveness.

REAL YOU

When I'm tempted to think more highly of myself than I ought, I'll consider Jesus' words. This is what he's done for me:

_____

_____

_____

_____

_____

_____

_____

_____

_____

_____

_____

_____

_____

_____

_____

As I reflect on Jesus' forgiveness, I also want to consider what's hardest for me to believe about the truth that "all have sinned." Here are three areas in my life where I continually need Jesus' grace and forgiveness:

_____

_____

_____

_____

_____

_____

_____

_____

_____

_____

_____

_____

_____

_____

_____

_____

_____

_____

_____

_____

_____

_____

_____

_____

_____

_____

Xalted

Righteous Servant

Only Jesus was good enough to be the
once-for-all, one-time sacrifice. Jesus did
everything right. He's the only one who can
make us "good" enough to stand before God.
Isaiah 53:11 assures us that Jesus, the "righteous servant," bore all our sins. He didn't come to do his own
will. He came to do God's will, as a good servant does. His ser-
vanthood is an example for us to follow.

I find the Jesus Experience when I extend forgiveness, unconditionally and completely.

"But when you are praying, first forgive anyone you are holding a grudge against, so that your Father in heaven will forgive your sins, too."

Mark 11:25

REAL XPRESSIONS

Forgiven or Unforgiven?

Janice made me feel guilty yet again. Way to go Jan. Not that I don't deserve it. After all, I *did* steal her boyfriend Chris from her. I don't know what I was thinking. I didn't know she was so into him.

Who am I kidding? I did know. They had been dating for about a month when I realized that I liked him too. Small world, huh? Turns out he liked me more than he liked Jan. So he asked me out. I never thought I'd do something like that to a friend—especially Jan. We've known each other since the third grade. We're both juniors now. We even go to the same church. But I did.

Chris and I weren't a couple for long though. After a month he decided he liked someone else at our high school. What a jerk! He couldn't leave soon enough!

Jan didn't speak to me for the rest of our sophomore year. I didn't blame her. I betrayed our friendship.

After Chris and I broke up, I came to my senses and asked Jan to forgive me. I must've apologized like 50 times. I hated losing her friendship. Most of all, I knew I needed to get right with God. It took a while, but she said she forgave me. I didn't think she would. When we started our junior year, it was like sophomore year hadn't happened.

Things are cool for the most part. But every once in a while Jan brings up what I did. She'll say stuff like, "If I get a new boyfriend, you'd better not try to steal him." She always says she's just teasing me. She usually does that right before she asks me for a favor, like borrowing a CD she likes or something. I never say no. I mean, I guess I still owe her.

The other day I was reading in the Psalms and turned to Psalm 51. I could really relate to that psalm. David wrote it after he stole another man's wife. As I was reading it's like I could sense that God was near. At least I know God forgives me. I'm still not sure that Jan really does.

Meredith

ReaL QUESTION

According to Jesus, does a person still owe something if she's been forgiven?

When you did something that hurt a friendship, you felt awful, didn't you? We've all said or done things that we wish we could press rewind and take back. If we're believers, we know that our actions not only harm our relationship with the person we've hurt, they also harm our relationship with God.

Sin creates a debt that needs to be paid. Until forgiveness is offered and accepted, that debt remains unresolved. Meredith's actions created a debt. How does Jan cause Meredith to feel guilty? Do you think Janice really forgave Meredith? Do you think Meredith forgives herself? Is it possible to forgive someone and not be phony about it? Can you forgive someone, even if you don't feel like it?

ReaL answer

You know the drill. Forgive and you will be forgiven. Jesus stated this plainly: "If you forgive those who sin against you, your heavenly Father will forgive you. But if you refuse to forgive others, your Father will not forgive your sins" (Matthew 6:14-15; see also 18:35). There's no middle ground when it comes to forgiveness. You either forgive a person or you don't forgive. To forgive is to cancel a debt. The forgiven person no longer owes anything.

Jesus told a parable about a servant who refused to forgive. That story is found in Matthew 18:23-35. First, the servant was forgiven a huge debt that he owed a king. He owed the king millions of dollars. The king felt sorry for him and canceled his debt. That meant that the servant did not owe anything—no secret tax or debt canceling fees. He owed nothing more. But he refused to forgive someone who owed him only a few thousand dollars. When the king found out about the servant's unforgiveness, he had the man thrown into prison until he could pay his original debt.

Jesus used that parable to stress the fact that God has forgiven the huge debt that we owed him. Because of the forgiveness made possible by Jesus' death, we can forgive each other. True forgiveness, however, doesn't mean bringing up the past. God purposely decides not to remind us of sins that he has forgiven. "He has removed our rebellious acts as far away from us as the east is from the west" (Psalm 103:12). "I will never again remember their sins and lawless deeds" (Hebrews 10:17). He expects us to do the same.

REAL YOU

To truly experience Jesus' forgiveness, I need to seek out the
following person or people to whom
I owe a debt:

_____

_____

_____

_____

_____

_____

_____

_____

_____

_____

_____

_____

_____

_____

_____

_____

To truly experience Jesus' forgiveness, I need to cancel the debt(s) of the following person or people:

_____

_____

_____

_____

_____

_____

_____

_____

_____

_____

_____

_____

_____

_____

_____

_____

_____

_____

_____

_____

_____

_____

_____

_____

ΧALTED

Good Hope

What do you hope for? A brand-new
car on your 16th birthday? A $1,000
shopping spree? A free ride to college? For
most of us, those are just illusions. Real hope
only comes in the person of Jesus Christ. None of
us would have any hope without Jesus. That's why
2 Thessalonians 2:16 describes him as our "hope." Because of
Jesus, God freely forgives us. Without Jesus, we have no chance of
God's forgiveness. Because of Jesus, we can live without fear, even when
we go through tough times. That's hope.

W hat makes you happy? Getting everything you want? Being popular? Getting into the best school? Having lots and lots of money? Having for a girlfriend or boyfriend the girl or guy everyone wants? Having "the right" clothes? Living someone else's life? Being attractive?

HAPPINESS AND SUCCESS

Some would say that happiness comes from what you have or what you look like. According to a recent Gallup poll, a whopping seven out of ten Americans stated that "physical attractiveness is important in society today 'in terms of . . . happiness, social life, and the ability to get ahead.'" How would you vote?

The search for happiness is an elusive road. Everyone's definition of success or happiness varies. Just when you think you've got it, something else grabs your attention. Does happiness equal success and success equal happiness? Success is defined as achieving something desired, planned, or attempted. To be happy means, "enjoying, showing, or marked by pleasure, satisfaction, or joy." For many people, satisfaction comes when they have achieved a goal. That's why many people think that they can only be happy if they've achieved success.

Society's views about what makes a person happy change from year to year. Just look at the commercials or print ads. If you don't have the latest car, lipstick, designer outfit, computer, TV, soft drink—whatever is being advertised, you won't be happy! You definitely won't be successful!

You can also see those same commercials or read a magazine to see how society views success. The magazines with the "100 most powerful people" provide a clue. Money, looks, fame, education are some of the ingredients for success, according to the world. Those desires may be on your list. But how would Jesus define success? Would he value the same characteristics? Read on.

DAY 16

I find the Jesus Experience when I buy into Jesus' definition of success.

"But the good soil represents honest, good-hearted people who hear God's message, cling to it, and steadily produce a huge harvest."

Luke 8:15

REAL XPRESSIONS

Fast Track

When I first started thinking about college, I had no idea what kind of school I'd want to go to. I looked at small schools, big schools, state schools, private schools, East Coast, Midwest—you name it. I didn't know enough to even start having an opinion. Every day, I got a ton of junk mail from colleges I'd never heard of. It's in one huge pile on the floor in my room.

We're hitting that stressful point in the year when we have to make a final decision. To make matters more intense, there's always been this unspoken competition between my friends and me. The other day, our econ teacher was talking about how fierce competition is for admissions. He told us to look around the room. "Here's your competition," he said. "Your best friend could edge you out of the school you want."

Ugly thought. It was bad enough that we were always trying to out-study each other or get the best grade on a test. Now it's gotten really bad. Instead of offering encouragement and suggestions, we make snide comments about other schools and act as if everyone else's choices are beneath us.

Somehow, all thoughts of God got lost in the mix. My focus had gone off in another direction. I had to take a serious look at where I was headed. Lately all I've thought about was whether or not I would get into the best school. I've completely disregarded what God might want for my life. I mean, I want to be successful and all, but without him, it's meaningless. I've been caught up in my pride, my own strength, and energy. But you know what? Any success I have comes only from him.

Ben

Real question

What does success mean
to Jesus?

Many Christians aren't sure how
they would answer that question. They
wonder whether or not God views human success as "sinful." Perhaps they've known people who
do whatever it takes to get ahead. "Whatever it takes"
might mean backstabbing a friend or compromising in some
way. You may know someone like that.

Others fear that God's view of a successful life is sitting around a
quiet monastery copying the Bible by hand. Would that appeal to you?
Oh, and by the way, when you go to the monastery, you lose your TV.

How do you think Ben will feel if he doesn't get into the college of his
choice but his friend does? How would you feel? What do you think Ben
understands about God's will for his life? How would that make his life
successful?

Real answer

According to today's standards, Jesus could be described
as unsuccessful. He didn't go to an Ivy
League school or any other college for that
matter. He didn't have a cell phone or an investment portfolio. Growing up in Nazareth wasn't cool.
In fact, one of Jesus' future disciples once exclaimed,
"Nazareth! Can anything good come from there?" (John 1:46).
The place was filled with thieves, low-life scum.

Jesus wasn't a "winner" even by Israelite standards. They wanted a
conquering hero for their Messiah. Jesus didn't come to lead an army to
victory over the Romans. He didn't come to earth to build a mighty kingdom, better than Solomon's. He was popular as long as he fed the crowds
fish and chips, but when he started saying tough things the crowd left
and his popularity dwindled (John 6:66-67).

Jesus came for one reason: to free people from sin. He accomplished
this by living a sinless life and going to the cross as our perfect sacrifice.
According to God's heavenly and eternal standards, his son was a complete success.

Jesus' obedience was "an example to follow" (John 13:15). As he once told his disciples, "You are my friends if you obey me" (John 15:14). To obey him may mean going against the flow of worldly success.

That's his idea of success. Is it yours?

REAL YOU

This is one area where I tend to put my own desires for success above those of Jesus:

_____

_____

_____

_____

_____

_____

_____

_____

_____

_____

_____

_____

_____

_____

_____

_____

_____

_____

_____

I need to adopt Jesus' definition of success into the following areas of my life:

_____

_____

_____

_____

_____

_____

_____

_____

_____

_____

_____

_____

_____

_____

_____

_____

_____

χALTED

Teacher

Have you ever impressed someone by what you know? Jesus often amazed people by his knowledge. He had no formal schooling beyond what kids in his culture were offered, but who needs formal schooling when you're the source of all wisdom? What are you willing to learn from the greatest teacher the world will ever know? "A student is not greater than the teacher. But the student who works hard will become like the teacher" (Luke 6:40).

I find the Jesus Experience when I am humble about the gifts God has given me.

"Anyone who welcomes a little child like this on my behalf welcomes me, and anyone who welcomes me welcomes my Father who sent me. Whoever is the least among you is the greatest."

Luke 9:48

REAL Xpressions

God-given Gifts

By the end of today, I will have been the subject of three more newspaper stories. Granted, one of those newspapers is my high school paper. But another is our city paper, and the third is a national newspaper. Not bad for a single day, right? That's what my life is like these days.

I'm a senior on the varsity track team. "J-Flash" is my nickname. I run the 400-meter race. I set a state record in the 400 at a meet last month. The newspaper called me the best runner in the state. (Hey, I'm just quoting the paper. Mom has this scrapbook filled with all the newspaper stories.) I have to admit that it's very flattering to have people ask me for autographs. Everyone makes a huge deal out of the way that I run.

Enough about me. That's been the problem lately. There's been so much hype about me that even I get caught up in it. Dad warned me not to let success go to my head. My little sister started making fun of me for thinking I was all that. I guess they were both right to remind me, but I still wasn't ready to listen.

After I set the 400 record, I started a new Bible study on the life of David. Even though King David had every reason to brag, he didn't. He just thanked God for the good gifts that God had given him. When I read David's story, I felt really convicted. Instead of praising God for giving me the ability to run, I'd been praising myself. Not good. I had to ask God's forgiveness for being pretty self-centered lately. It's good for me to acknowledge that I owe everything to the Lord—all of my success as a runner. I need to keep reminding myself of that.

Jonelle

Real Question

How does Jesus react when we get caught up in our success?

Muhammad Ali, a well-known heavy-weight champion, once referred to himself as "The Greatest." No self-esteem problems there! There was no question that he believed he was the greatest boxer ever. In fact, many people shared that view.

What are you good at? Make a quick list in your head. We'll wait. . . . Are you "the greatest" at what you do? You don't have to answer out loud. Everyone wants to be good at something. Some people even achieve greatness in their abilities. Look at Olympic athletes or Nobel prize-winning authors. But is greatness the only goal worth achieving?

If you were "J-Flash," how would you react to all of the hype? How would you keep from letting success go to your head? Why is it important to thank God for the gifts he has given? Do you know anyone whose ego gets in the way? How do you usually feel when you're around this person? Do you know anyone who is so full of himself, you want to throw up?

Real answer

Jesus has one word for the "J-Flashes" of this world: *humility.* During his time on earth, Jesus said a lot about humility. Even if he hadn't said anything, his actions and life spoke louder than words. One day he fell into a discussion with his disciples about the subject. What sparked it was the disciples' argument over who would be the greatest in heaven. They were often concerned about who would get the best seats in heaven. Jesus solved that argument by calling a child to his side. Whoever welcomed a child welcomed Jesus, he said. Then he said something surprising: "Whoever is the least among you is the greatest" (Luke 9:48). He also said, "Anyone who becomes as humble as this little child is the greatest in the Kingdom of Heaven" (Matthew 18:4). What is it about children that makes them so humble? They are innocent, teachable, and trusting. They know that they don't know everything, so they are willing to learn!

Humility, besides being the opposite of pride, is the ability to look away from self. It goes hand in hand with gratitude toward God for the gifts he has provided. In fact, a thankful attitude is a sign of humility. Knowing that God is the source of all good gifts is a great start. If you choose not to be humble about your God-given talents, then heed the warning of Proverbs 16:18, "Pride goes before destruction, and haughtiness before a fall."

REAL YOU

To experience Jesus, I need to first thank him for the gifts I've been given. Thank you, Lord, for ...

_____

_____

_____

_____

_____

_____

_____

_____

_____

_____

_____

_____

_____

_____

_____

_____

_____

_____

Starting today, I want to use my talents to do something for God. So I will . . .

_____

_____

_____

_____

_____

_____

_____

_____

_____

_____

_____

_____

_____

Χalted

Indescribable Gift

What's the best gift you have ever received? Some people would say that an ability they have or the way they look is the best gift. Some might even say that *they're* the best gift—God's gift to the world! God did offer the world a gift (besides you)—his Son. He is a gift too wonderful for words (2 Corinthians 9:15). Best of all, this is the gift that keeps on giving. Have you received this gift?

I find the Jesus Experience when I look first for satisfaction in a relationship with God.

"Why be like the pagans who are so deeply concerned about these things? Your heavenly Father already knows all your needs, and he will give you all you need from day to day if you live for him and make the Kingdom of God your primary concern."

Matthew 6:32-33

REAL Xpressions

A Dream Come True?

Imagine having your dream come true. You've finally got the perfect boyfriend who seems crazy about you.

I don't have to imagine that. It's a reality for me. I've liked Rich for two years. I first started liking him at the pep rally at school during my freshman year. (He was a sophomore then.) He's tall, smart, and absolutely gorgeous. Dark brown hair. Green eyes. Did I mention how nice he is? I knew I couldn't be happy without him.

I did everything I could to make sure I was everywhere he happened to be. At the wrestling team's matches (he's a wrestler), at the bowling alley near school. I even tried snowboarding because I knew he liked to do it. I was willing to do anything to get him. And when I say anything, I mean *anything.* I spent hours thinking about how I was going to get him to like me.

Once I started going out with him, all I could think about was being with him. That was cool for the first couple of months. But then I started worrying about whether or not we'd break up. I was surprised to also find that I really wasn't satisfied. It's not that I didn't like Rich. I just kept thinking: *Is this it?* I still didn't feel all that happy inside. I didn't know why at first.

Oddly enough, Rich was the one who helped me see why. Rich is a Christian. He thought I was. But I wasn't. At least, not right away. He had something I didn't have. I don't know how to describe it. I wasn't everything to him. It's like he didn't need me to be happy. I didn't realize that I'd been looking for something like that. Not until I went to his church. I thought I was going just because he asked me to go. It wasn't the first thing I wanted to do. I've been to church before, but my family doesn't go as often as Rich's.

At his church the guy preaching asked a question that caught my attention: "Are you happy?" A year ago, I would've said yes. I've finally got a boyfriend I really like. Now I know that's not entirely true. The speaker didn't stop there. He talked about how contentment is a gift of God. Only God could satisfy a person's deepest desires. Suddenly that made sense to me. That was what I wanted.

Lynnae

ReaL Question

Can Jesus really bring satisfaction to a person's life?

What is the one thing you want more than anything? (Be honest! Nobody's looking over your shoulder.) Now ask yourself this: Will the thing I'm seeking—even if it's a relationship with the most gorgeous, smartest, coolest person I know—fill all of the empty spaces in my life? If so, for how long?

Listen to the radio, and undoubtedly you will hear a love song. There's one playing somewhere every second or so. Everyone's looking for love somewhere. When you find it, you hope that the relationship will satisfy all your deepest needs, don't you? (Or at least, you dream it will.)

What did Lynnae expect from Rich? Was a relationship with him all that she hoped for? Can you relate to Lynnae? If you were a friend of Lynnae and heard her discuss her strategy for "snagging" Rich, what would you say to her?

ReaL answer

A lot of people are hungry. But not just for food. They're starved for meaningful companionship. They're starved for love. For attention. For belonging.

That's why worry sometimes sets in. People wonder if they'll find the right girlfriend or boyfriend or whether or not they'll ever marry. During his Sermon on the Mount, Jesus warned his listeners not to worry, but instead to "live for [God] and make the Kingdom of God your primary concern" (Matthew 6:33). In other words, make honoring him your first priority.

Does that mean you shouldn't date? There's nothing wrong with dating. It's when it becomes the number one priority in your life that trouble starts. The same is true with whatever you pursue, whether it's college, success on the athletic field, or a career. Any of these can quickly bump God out of first place in your life if you don't actively choose to give him first place.

The world tells you to go after what you want, when you want it, however you can get it. If scheming works, then scheme away. But Jesus said to seek God first. Only God can make a person truly satisfied. This contentment can keep you from feeling discouraged when you can't get a date, or don't get into your first choice for college, or don't get that "dream" job. Unless Jesus is part of your life's plan, nothing you achieve or acquire will truly make your life full.

Need some satisfaction? "Seek the LORD while you can find him. Call on him now while he is near" (Isaiah 55:6). He will never disappoint you.

REAL YOU

In order to experience the fullness of my relationship with Jesus, I'll examine the relationships that have a higher priority than my relationship with God. They are:

_____

_____

_____

_____

_____

_____

_____

_____

_____

_____

_____

_____

_____

_____

_____

_____

I want to show that the kingdom of God is my first priority. Here are a few steps I can take:

_____

_____

_____

_____

_____

_____

_____

_____

_____

_____

_____

_____

_____

_____

_____

_____

Xalted

Messiah

Imagine waiting 700 years for something. (And you thought waiting in line for the latest blockbuster movie took forever.) The promised Savior's arrival happened 700 years after the prophets Isaiah and Micah foretold his coming. This Savior was called by the Hebrew term *Messiah*, which means "anointed one" (Matthew 16:15-16). He would "save his people from their sins" (Matthew 1:21). Jesus fulfilled all of the promises associated with the Messiah. Only he can satisfy a life for all eternity. Are you looking to Jesus to meet your needs today and forever?

DAY 19

I find the Jesus Experience when I trust in God's future for me.

"I assure you, if you have faith and don't doubt, you can do things like this and much more. You can even say to this mountain, 'May God lift you up and throw you into the sea,' and it will happen."

Matthew 21:21

REAL Xpressions

Sidelined

I guess the new associate pastor thought he was encouraging me a couple weeks ago when he came to see me in the hospital and wrote "Romans 8:28" in big black letters across the top of my cast.

I knew what the verse was when he wrote it, but I didn't say anything. It's that one about all things working together for good for people who love God. Church people love to go around quoting it when bad things happen.

You want to talk about all things working together? Try this: Starting quarterback for the number-two ranked team in the state. Highest quarterback rating in the conference. College scouts coming to see me even though I'm a junior. Scholarship offers. Three touchdown passes in the first quarter against Beech Grove.

Blown-out knee on the first play of the second quarter.

That's the way things have "worked together" for me that week. When the X-rays came back, the doctor told me that I had a torn ACL and a severely sprained MCL, which is a medical way of saying, "If you do ever play again, you'll never be as good. Kiss your scholarships good-bye."

I'm trying hard not to doubt God. But right now, I just don't see how he can make something good come from this. But God must be working in me because I keep staring at that verse the associate pastor wrote on my cast. I keep thinking about what it means to trust him in this situation.

So that's my new strategy—watching, waiting, and wondering what God can do with someone with one good leg.

Flint

REAL QUESTION

What can Jesus do when your dreams go down the drain?

Ever wish you could order life off a menu? "I'll take an easy life with a side order of fries, please." Unfortunately, life doesn't always work out neatly. Bad things happen. Some of these are nightmares beyond our wildest imagination.

When hard times come, doubt often comes along for the ride. Many people wonder how a loving God could allow rain to spoil their parade.

What is the worst disaster you have ever faced? Did you ever imagine that anything good could come of it? When tough times come, what do you expect from God? Imagine you're Flint lying in that hospital bed. Playing football was all you ever wanted to do. What do you think of when you see the "Romans 8:28" on your cast? If you were Flint's friend, what would you say to him?

REAL ANSWER

Imagine being born on this earth knowing:

- You will never marry.
- You will never have children.
- You will bear the sorrows of the world.
- You will be misunderstood most of the time.
- You will hardly ever be thanked for anything you do.
- One of your closest friends will betray you.

Welcome to Jesus' life. It wasn't an easy one. The worst disaster of all was about to happen to him after the last supper. He knew that he would be arrested and suffer an agonizing death. He was only 33. Not exactly what the typical thirty-something today has in mind for the "ideal" life.

While in the garden of Gethsemane, he told his disciples, "My soul is crushed with grief to the point of death" (Matthew 26:38). He prayed, asking God if there was any way for the cup to pass from him (Matthew 26:42). The answer was no. He had to go through with it.

Because of God's mercy, there's good news, even when things look worst. "The LORD is close to the brokenhearted; he rescues those who are crushed in spirit" (Psalm 34:18).

This promise can help you hang on. When troubles come, you can repeat with Paul: "We are pressed on every side by troubles, but we are not crushed and broken. We are perplexed, but we don't give up and quit" (2 Corinthians 4:8).

When we truly trust Jesus, we lay our plans at his feet, acknowledging that he is in control. He knows what is best for us, even if it doesn't make sense at the time.

REAL YOU

When I think about my future this is what I hope will happen:

_____

_____

_____

_____

_____

_____

_____

_____

_____

_____

_____

_____

_____

_____

One way that I've seen Romans 8:28 in action is when this occurred:

_____

_____

_____

_____

_____

_____

_____

_____

_____

_____

_____

_____

_____

_____

Xalted

Lion of the Tribe of Judah

Think about a lion, the king of beasts. What attributes come to mind? Strength, power, authority, majesty. All these characteristics of a lion are evident in the work and life of Jesus. When Jesus, the Lion of Judah, rules in your life, you have access to all the strength, power, and authority that has been given to him (Revelation 5:5). With Jesus at your side, your future is secure in him. That's why you can trust him to work out all things in your life for good.

I find the Jesus Experience when I'm more concerned with the way I look inside than outside.

"Beware of these teachers of religious law! For they love to parade in flowing robes and to have everyone bow to them as they walk in the marketplaces. And how they love the seats of honor in the synagogues and at banquets. But they shamelessly cheat widows out of their property, and then, to cover up the kind of people they really are, they make long prayers in public. Because of this, their punishment will be the greater."

Luke 20:46-47

REAL Xpressions

Looking Good . . . Inside

Erica, Alexis, Faith, and I are best friends.
We've grown up together and gone through everything together—the braces phase, the ugly hair phase,
the bad attitude phase, the boy-crazy phase, and even the
divorced parents phase. When you have that kind of history
with your friends, you know you're tight. I guess you could say that
we're in a shopping phase now. It's fun to shop together, but it can put
a strain on our friendships. Like, if Faith buys a new outfit, then we all feel
like we've got to get something, too. It's an unspoken competition.

Last week, I was walking to history class with Erica. This girl Amber
stopped us in the hall. She's one of the most popular girls in our class.
Anyway, Amber started going on and on about how much she loved Erica's
outfit, asking where she got it, saying how cool it was, etc., etc., etc. It
actually kind of bothered me. Her outfit was nothing special, and Amber
acted like she didn't notice what I was wearing. Even after we walked
away, I kept thinking about it all during class.

That evening, I asked Dad if I could borrow some money for shopping.
I'd already spent all the money I made from my job. Well, Dad went ballistic! He snapped about how I spend way too much money on clothes and
how I was so wrapped up in my appearance. His reaction caught me off
guard. I mean yeah, I like to shop and everything, but I didn't think I was
obsessing about clothes and how I look. It got me thinking, too.

The Holy Spirit started convicting me that night. He reminded me of
a verse I'd memorized in youth group, about how God looks at a person's
heart. Maybe I have been putting too much emphasis on how I look.

Tiffany

REAL QUESTION

Quiz time! Circle which you would prefer:

(a) To always know what styles are cool and always have an updated wardrobe.

(b) To not have to worry about what's in style.

(c) I'm not sure.

If you picked (a), you've got lots of company. Many people wish they were in the know about what's hot and what's not. Not only that, they wish they had the big bucks to be on the top of the fashion chain, rather than on the "fashion police" list. For some the desire is so strong, it makes them miserable.

No one wants to be thought of as a fashion failure.

Have you ever judged a person by what he or she had on? Have you ever thought, *If I don't have the right clothes, hairstyle, _____ I can't be happy?* (Fill in the blank.) But what happens on a bad hair day?

If you were Tiffany, what would you say to your friends about the unspoken competition? When have you seen something like this happen among your friends? What did you do?

REAL ANSWER

Jesus preached part of his Sermon on the Mount on a subject that hits everyone: worry. He explained, "Life consists of far more than food and clothing" (Luke 12:23). He knew that worry was a burden that no one could handle. He followed that up with this: "So don't worry about having enough food or drink or clothing. Why be like the pagans who are so deeply concerned about these things? Your heavenly Father already knows all your needs" (Matthew 6:31-32).

Jesus knew the thoughts of the people. The most judgmental of all were the Pharisees. They wore the coolest robes—the kind with long tassels (Hey! They were cool back in the day!)—because they wanted everyone to think that they were very "spiritual." He once told them off because they were so careful to be clean on the outside. (See Matthew 23:25-28.)

But their filth on the inside was a totally different matter. According to Jesus, "they shamelessly cheat widows out of their property, and then, to cover up the kind of people they really are, they make long prayers in public" (Luke 20:47). Not good! It didn't fool God back then, and those types of "shows" don't fool God now, either.

Centuries before Jesus came, the Lord told the prophet Samuel, "The LORD doesn't make decisions the way you do! People judge by outward appearance, but the LORD looks at a person's thoughts and intentions" (1 Samuel 16:7). What would he say about your "thoughts and intentions"?

REAL YOU

I tend to make snap judgments about people based on the following:

_____

_____

_____

_____

_____

_____

_____

_____

_____

_____

_____

_____

_____

_____

_____

I'm convinced that what really counts in God's eyes are these things . . .

_____

_____

_____

_____

_____

_____

_____

_____

_____

_____

_____

_____

_____

_____

_____

Xalted

The One Who Lifts My Head

What gets you down? What tops your list
of worries? Worry, fear, anxiety, and guilt can
work to keep our heads bowed low and our focus
on ourselves and our immediate situation. So
what's the solution? Listen to the psalmist's words,
"But you, O Lord, are a shield around me, my glory, and the
one who lifts my head high" (Psalm 3:3). In Bible times, to lift a
person's head meant to accept that person, or even to exalt that person.

Who is this one who lifts our head? None other than Jesus. Keep your
focus on Jesus, who is above all your circumstances and worries and who
accepts you unconditionally!

I find the Jesus Experience when I choose to obey, rather than compromise.

"And how do you benefit if you gain the whole world but lose your own soul in the process?"

Mark 8:36

REAL χpressions

The Golden Opportunity

Two months ago, Maya and her friends didn't even know who I was. They never looked at me in the hall or talked to me in class. And now? Well, let's just say that I know a lot of girls who wish they would have gotten invited to Maya's house for the weekend.

Like I did.

That's right, Maya asked me herself. She's having a sleepover, and she wants me to come! If you're wondering how that happened, I guess it's just a matter of being in the right place at the right time. At the beginning of this semester, Maya and I got paired up in science lab. I don't think she was too happy about it at first. But then we started talking about music one day in class, and we just hit it off. After that, she started waving to me whenever she saw me. Then her friends started waving, too. It's like I'm one of them.

Now all I have to do is make my parents understand. When I told them about the party, they said what they always say: "No." They said they weren't comfortable with the idea because they didn't know Maya's parents.

They have no clue what this could mean for me. They don't understand that you only get a few chances to become popular in high school. They don't care about what might happen if I tell Maya I can't go. I tried to explain it to them, but I couldn't make them see how important this is to me.

This is one of those times when I wish I could rewrite the Bible. I'd start with that stuff about honoring your parents.

Ellie

REAL QUESTION

Is there anything wrong
with wanting to be popular?

Do you have to be popular to be
happy? What would you do in order to make
that happen?

Let's face it. Many people would give their right
arm to be popular. There's nothing like walking into a
place and having everyone know who you are. You get invited
to the best parties that way! Everybody wants to talk to you. You
would never have to face a weekend at home alone. But what if being
popular meant you had to do something wrong?

How would you feel if you were Ellie? What would you say to your parents to try to convince them to let you go? What would you say to Maya if you couldn't go? If you were Ellie's friend, what would you say to her?

REAL ANSWER

If Jesus talked to
Ellie, maybe he would say
this: "How do you benefit if you
gain the whole world but lose your own
soul in the process? Is anything worth more
than your soul?" (Mark 8:36-37.) Sounds drastic,
but Jesus wanted to make a drastic point. Is what
you're seeking worth compromising? A little bit of compromise can go a long way. Maybe Ellie would "gain the whole
world" by being popular. But she might lose something in return.

Jesus also said, "If any of you wants to be my follower, you must put aside your selfish ambition, shoulder your cross, and follow me" (Mark 8:34). What does it mean to "shoulder your cross"? Are there things you need to die to, like maybe wanting to be popular no matter what the cost? Is following Jesus more important than doing what you want?

Is wanting to be popular so wrong? Not necessarily. During the first year of his ministry, Jesus was more popular than sliced bread. (OK, they didn't have sliced bread then, but you get the point.) Everyone wanted to listen to him and see his miracles. Yet that popularity didn't last. He wound up going to the cross at the request of a large crowd of people.

Being popular isn't wrong. But how you get there could be. And if you want popularity just for the sake of having it, even if popularity means disobeying God in some way, you're headed for trouble.

REAL YOU

A time when I was willing to do anything *but* obey God was this:

_____

_____

_____

_____

_____

_____

_____

_____

_____

_____

_____

_____

_____

_____

_____

_____

_____

_____

_____

_____

_____

_____

_____

To experience Jesus, I need to lay aside any desire I have that would cause me to compromise what I believe about him. That means I need to get rid of these things:

_____

_____

_____

_____

_____

_____

_____

_____

_____

_____

_____

_____

_____

_____

_____

_____

_____

_____

Xalted

Glory of Israel

The "glory" of a person often comes from that which makes someone feel important or gives him or her significance. A parent may find "glory" in a child's achievements. A businessman may find glory in his title or accomplishments. For the people of Israel, their glory was reflected in their unique relationship to the one true God. And although many Jews did not recognize it, Jesus came to be Israel's crowning glory (Luke 2:32).

So what makes you feel important? Is it who you know? Is it what you own, or have achieved? Or is it your relationship with Jesus?

I find the Jesus Experience when I put Jesus ahead of the stuff in my life.

"Yes, a person is a fool to store up earthly wealth but not have a rich relationship with God."

Luke 12:21

REAL χPRESSIONS

Stuffaholic

My name is Trudy. I'm a stuffaholic.
That may sound funny to you, but it's no joke.
I have the biggest CD collection of my friends. I've
been collecting these ceramic angels since I was a kid.
I have so many I needed a cabinet just for them. Then
there's my jewelry. Don't get me started on that.

I'm not bragging about my stuff. Well, I used to. No lie. At first it was fun to collect the angels, the CDs, and jewelry. It was even cool to be known around the school as the "Queen of Stuff." Then after a while, the stuff started taking over my life. (It already had taken over my room!) I started worrying about how I was going to get the money to add to my collections. I worried when the latest CD came out how quickly I could get to the store. I spent hours pouring over magazines and catalogues to check out the latest in rings and anklet bracelets.

My mom's been saying all along that I have too much stuff! Instead of getting more shelves or boxes or cabinets, I needed to get rid of some of my collections. Well, I kind of ignored what she said. It wasn't until I helped out in the little kids' Sunday school class two weeks ago that I got a wake-up call.

See, Mrs. Murphy (the teacher—I'm her assistant) was telling the three- and four-year-olds about a widow who put in two coins in the temple—all of the money she had. Jesus lifted her up as an example. He said that she had given more than anyone. And I get upset if someone just asks to borrow one CD!

But that's not all that really hit me. The story next week was about a rich guy who came to Jesus for advice. Jesus told him to sell all that he had and give to the poor. I remember thinking that there was no way I could give up all the stuff I had, even if Jesus asked me. And that's when it hit me. My possessions had a higher priority than Jesus.

Trudy

REAL QUESTION

Does your stuff get in the way of your relationship with Jesus?

How much do you need to be happy? Can a person ever have too much? According to the ads you see daily, some would answer that question with a big no. There's always a new CD, video, DVD, bracelet, running shoe, car, Ginzu knife, etc. that you've just *gotta* have.

Most people aren't sure where Jesus stands on the "stuff" issue. After all, the culture during Bible times was far different from ours. People didn't have as busy a lifestyle as we have. That's why they feel that the gadgets available today are totally necessary to the way we live. How would you respond to that?

If you were Trudy's friend, what would you want to say to her about her possessions? If Jesus were in her room looking at all of her collections, what do you think he would say?

REAL ANSWER

A guy who wanted his share of the family estate approached Jesus one day. You can find the story in Luke 12:13-21. In other words, he wanted more "stuff." He expected Jesus to side with him about his need for the money. But instead Jesus replied, "Don't be greedy for what you don't have. Real life is not measured by how much we own." He followed that up with a parable about a rich farmer. Talk about a guy who had it all. This guy had so many crops, he decided to build bigger barns to house them all. But God had a surprise for him. The farmer was scheduled to die that night! All that time spent gathering "stuff" was all for nothing. He wasn't going to be able to take it all with him!

So, what was Jesus' point? Was he saying that having possessions is bad? No. Was he saying that you shouldn't ever buy a new CD or clothes? No. The point was that there is more to life than just having material things. "A rich relationship with God" (Luke 12:21) is worth more than a whole barn full of stuff. You can't have that if you're worried about how much you have or don't have. Check out the rest of what Jesus said in Luke 12:22-31. He may not always meet our wants, but he will meet our needs.

Maybe you've seen the bumper sticker that says, "He who dies with the most toys . . . still dies." It's really true. And, the way we spend our money shows what we value. "Wherever your treasure is, there your heart and thoughts will also be" (Luke 12:34).

After all, when we die, our possessions stay here!

REAL YOU

When I think about the possessions in my life this is what comes to mind:

_____

_____

_____

_____

_____

_____

_____

_____

_____

_____

_____

_____

_____

_____

_____

_____

_____

_____

_____

_____

Here are some steps I can take so that my "stuff" doesn't get in the way of my relationship with Jesus:

_____

_____

_____

_____

_____

_____

_____

_____

_____

_____

_____

_____

_____

_____

_____

_____

_____

Χalted

Life

Get a life! No doubt, you've heard
that expression before. Usually, it's
directed at someone who has invested exces-
sive amounts of time in something trivial, like
mastering the latest computer game or memoriz-
ing the lines to a favorite movie.

It's so easy to become preoccupied with stuff that doesn't
matter. But real life is so much more than that, and it is found only
in Christ, who is the Life (John 14:16). Through him you can know the realities of heaven and the joys that go beyond what you can see and touch
here on earth. Look beyond what you can see and set your sights on
Christ and get "real" life that comes from him.

I find the Jesus Experience when I use my talents for his glory.

"To those who use well what they are given, even more will be given, and they will have an abundance. But from those who are unfaithful, even what little they have will be taken away."

Matthew 25:29

REAL Xpressions

College Daze

Whenever my parents send me e-mails at school, the "Subject" heading is always the same: "Don't You Ever Study?" It's a running joke because they say whenever I talk about what's going on at school or what I've been doing lately, I never mention classes or professors or work or anything.

They don't understand that, for me, classes are just a small part of what college is all about. It's not like I'm blowing off my work, either. My GPA was 3.8 first semester, and it's probably going to go up this semester. That puts me on track to graduate magna cum laude, which will look great on my résumé.

What can I say? I picked the right major. My classes are a breeze, so I have a lot of time to goof around. Not like the pre-med geek who lives down the hall. We call him "The Ghost" because he only comes out of his room late at night, after he's done studying. I couldn't live like that. I'd die without a social life.

But I do understand what my parents are talking about. My dad asked me a question in his last e-mail message that really got me thinking. He wrote in capital letters, "ARE YOU TAKING ADVANTAGE OF EVERY OPPORTUNITY YOU HAVE IN COLLEGE?"

And I realized that the answer is no, I'm not. I've been using my good grades as an excuse for watching a lot of TV, playing a lot of video games, and just hanging out with my friends.

But that's like saying, "God made me smart, so I don't have to use my brain." And that makes no sense at all. So, to use Jesus' words, maybe it's time I started taking the "much" I've been given and doing "much" with it.

Brent

REAL QUESTION

How can we know what God wants us to do with our abilities?

Many people talk about the "American Dream." What's your definition of it? For some, it's winning the lottery. Free money (aside from the taxes) can mean bye-bye to 9-to-5 drudgery.

For others, it might mean not having to work very hard. It could mean just doing enough to get by. "A 'C' or a 'D' is good enough for me." It might also require taking a job that doesn't use any of your abilities—just one to pay the rent and that's all.

In Brent's case, it meant coasting on his GPA. Do you think that success means having things come easily? Think about how you'd feel if you were Brent. How would you respond to your dad's e-mail? If you were Brent's roommate, what advice would you have for him?

REAL answer

Jesus told a parable about some money a master gave to his servants. He expected them to invest his money while he left on a trip. (Check out Matthew 25:14-30.) One guy received five talents, another two, and a third one. A talent was a unit of money. To make a long story short, the ones entrusted with the five and two talents made five more and two more respectively. The guy with the one talent took the easy way out and buried his. Brent was like that guy.

When the master returned, he rewarded the two servants for their creative use of the talents. The guy with the one talent had that talent taken away. So, is this just a story about some foreign money? No. This story is a strong encouragement to put to use the talents or abilities God has given. "To those who use well what they are given, even more will be given, and they will have an abundance" (Matthew 25:29). Using your talents can lead to the development of other talents. Perhaps you have a gift for music. That might enable you to play different kinds of instruments. But you'll never discover that if you don't put your talent to use. Get the picture?

Everyone has a talent of some kind. (Being critical is *not* a talent.) Maybe you can't paint like Michelangelo. Maybe your drawings make a kindergartner's look like something Michelangelo did by comparison. But you can do something. Maybe you're good at encouraging others. Maybe you're great at shopping for bargains. Maybe you're great at sports. You can use whatever you're good at to bring God glory.

So, what is success? It's using what God gave you to the fullest. It's making the most of every opportunity. To put it another way, use it or lose it!

REAL YOU

These are some of the talents
I have:

_____

_____

_____

_____

_____

_____

_____

_____

_____

_____

_____

_____

_____

_____

_____

_____

_____

_____

_____

_____

_____

_____

These are some of the ways I'm using my talents to bring glory to God:

_____

_____

_____

_____

_____

_____

_____

_____

_____

_____

_____

_____

_____

_____

_____

_____

_____

Xalted

David

David was quite a guy. He devoted
his life to using his gifts and abilities
for God's glory. Take a look at the short list
of his résumé: Shepherd. Musician. Songwriter.
Administrator. Architect. King. In Ezekiel 37:24, the
Messiah was referred to as David, since he was from
David's family line. The human David, though, was not perfect.
Only the heavenly David, Jesus, came to perfectly use his talents and
abilities to bring glory to his Father.

As followers of this David, we, too, are called to bring glory to the
Father by using the gifts and abilities he has given to us.

Fear. Everyone has felt that heart-racing, throat-drying, skin-tingling, knee-knocking feeling. With terrorist attacks, war, unemployment, illnesses, and other issues in the news or at home, fear is part of our daily lives. A feeling of safety can sometimes seem out of reach.

fear and security

Fear comes in many flavors. There's the fear of change, the fear of death, the fear of spiders, the fear of the future—you name it. Everyone's got a phobia of some kind.

Security is the flip side to fear. Let's face it—we all need to feel secure. Think about what makes you feel most secure. When you were a little kid afraid to go to sleep at night, knowing that a parent was nearby probably made you feel secure. That and your favorite blanket! Now that you're older, maybe that blanket doesn't cut it anymore. Maybe you've moved on to bigger "blankets" (besides the electric kind). Maybe your GPA and college scholarship make you feel secure. Maybe your family's status and income or your *own* status and income make you feel secure. Maybe an SUV gives you that feeling of security as you cruise the roads laughing at smaller vehicles. Maybe you lean toward the military might or the police force to make you feel secure. Or maybe, you feel big enough and strong enough to not need anything external to make you feel secure. Yet, none of these things can make you feel secure forever.

The good news though, is that in a world that sometimes seems like an unending war movie, long-lasting security is possible. Where can you get this kind of security? It's found under only one name:

Jesus.

How is that possible? Keep reading.

I find the Jesus Experience when I look to him for protection.

"I am the good shepherd; I know my own sheep, and they know me, just as my Father knows me and I know the Father. And I lay down my life for the sheep."

John 10:14-15

real χpressions

Strange Comfort

Graham and I are just so different. He's only a year older than I am, but we are nothing alike. I'm outgoing and like to be around my friends all the time, and he's a total loner. He's in this silent phase. He hardly talks to anyone now, not even our mom.

Sometimes Graham scares me. I hate to be alone with him. Sometimes it's fine, and we just do our own things. But other times, he blows up. He goes into a rage for no reason and then lashes out at me. Last weekend, we were just chatting about school, and he stormed across the room, grabbed me and threw me down on the floor, and started kicking me in the ribs. He swore at me and said this is what I got for thinking I'm better than he is. Another time he pinned me up against the wall and squeezed my wrists so hard I started to cry. My wrists were so bruised that I had to wear long sleeves for a week. He's hit me lots of times, but I can't tell anyone. He said that if I ever say anything, he'd really hurt me.

Sometimes I feel so alone, like I'm the only one who's ever gone through this. God gives some strange comfort, though. The other day I read Cain and Abel's story again, and it hit me how much our situation is like theirs. Talk about a violent brother! It was so comforting to realize that God sees me, and he knows what I'm going through. He's my protector. I've been praying about whether or not I should say something about Graham. I think I should. I think my mom might suspect something's not right because she always tries to take me with her when she leaves the house. Mom's not perfect, but I think she'll have some answers. It's strange comfort, but I'm never really alone.

Amie

real question

Does Jesus really care
when we don't feel safe?

Home is supposed to be this
secure place. As Dorothy said at the end of
The Wizard of Oz, "There's no place like home."
But some homes are anything but safe. Relationships
with troubled family members can make home a living
nightmare.

Amie probably felt that way about Graham—she didn't have to
do or say anything to set him off. Being around Graham was like walking on eggshells. She felt alone and afraid. Maybe she wondered whether
she could even trust her mom to do something about Graham. Think
about how you would feel if you were Amie. What would you do or say to
Graham? What would you say to your mom about him? What would you
expect God to do in this situation?

real answer

Imagine having a son who
wanted you dead.

King David didn't have to imagine
what that was like. He lived with the reality. His son Absalom wanted to take over the
throne of Israel. David was warned to escape or be
killed. He wrote Psalm 3 while on the run from Absalom
and his army.

David was used to the idea of running for his life. In previous
years, a jealous King Saul wanted him dead. David barely managed to
stay one step ahead of Saul, and fear and a racing heart were his close
companions for several years. But knowing that God was his shepherd
helped him deal with his fear. It takes a shepherd to know a shepherd.
David, a former shepherd, recognized that God was his place of security.
He even wrote a psalm about it—Psalm 23.

Centuries later, a descendant of David would come to earth as the ultimate shepherd. Jesus was described as "the great Shepherd of the sheep"
(Hebrews 13:20). Shortly before his arrest, Jesus prayed that his disciples
would be protected and cared for. He spoke of his shepherd's care:

"During my time here, I have kept them safe. I guarded them" (John 17:12). After his death, Jesus sent the Holy Spirit to watch over his disciples and other believers yet to join the sheepfold. Jesus knew that they would face trouble and persecution. He even reminded them of that: "Here on earth you will have many trials and sorrows" (John 16:33). That was strange comfort indeed! But the good news was that God would be with them.

You can't run from some fearful situations or relationships. They're unfair, and worst of all, they're a daily reality. But don't forget—God cares. When you are in a tough situation, look to your shepherd, Jesus, for protection.

ReaL YOU

Because I know that Jesus wants to be my main place of security, I need to examine the people, places, or things that I've always believed were secure in my life. Here are the things in my life that I count on more than I count on Jesus:

_____

_____

_____

_____

_____

_____

_____

_____

_____

_____

_____

_____

_____

_____

_____

_____

_____

_____

_____

_____

Because I know that God is my protector, I can take something that makes me fearful and hand it to him. I can trust that he is big enough to handle any situation that comes my way. Here's one situation where I need Jesus to protect me:

_____

_____

_____

_____

_____

_____

_____

_____

_____

_____

_____

_____

_____

_____

_____

Xalted

Shepherd of Israel

The psalm writer, Asaph, pleaded with the "Shepherd of Israel" (Psalm 80:1) to "come to rescue us!" What did they need rescuing from? The psalm was written after the destruction of the Northern Kingdom of Israel. The people had suffered during that time. They desperately needed to hear from God. They wanted him to rescue them from their enemies.

God is called a shepherd in a number of passages of Scripture (for example, Psalm 23:1 and John 10:11). For the people of Israel, the shepherd image was a comforting one. A good shepherd protected his sheep. Best of all, a good shepherd anticipated and provided for the needs of his sheep. Think of Jesus as your shepherd. You might cross out Israel above and insert your own name. "Shepherd of _____." It's got a nice ring to it, doesn't it?

I find the Jesus Experience when I model Jesus to others through my leadership.

"You call me 'Teacher' and 'Lord,' and you are right, because it is true. And since I, the Lord and Teacher, have washed your feet, you ought to wash each other's feet. I have given you an example to follow. Do as I have done to you."

John 13:13-15

REAL Xpressions

Leader of the Pack

I hang around a bunch of guys *(mis amigos)* in my neighborhood. Most of us are sophomores. One guy's a freshman. (We don't hold that against him.) We've known each other since we were young.

We all kind of look up to one guy in particular—Jorge. He's a junior. He's the kind of guy who would do anything for you. And he's fun to be around. Usually Jorge will come up with plans or something fun for us to do, and we'll all go along with it. Normally, he's an incredible guy. But lately, I've had some doubts about him.

He's started to change some. He's been drinking. A lot. Some of the other guys in our group . . . well, they've been drinking too now because Jorge does. If Jorge does it, then it must be OK. Like I said, everybody follows him. But what he's doing isn't cool.

Last Saturday, for instance, eight of us were hanging out, shooting some hoops. Jorge and Diego arrived late. Both of them looked a little wasted. I wanted to say something to Jorge then, but I didn't want the guys to think I was preaching or something. Everybody knows that I'm *the Christian* of the group. (Maybe I should get a T-shirt made or something.) It's not that the other guys don't believe in God, but I'm the only one who really goes to church or tries to live for him.

This past Thursday, my small group discussed Nehemiah. I think it's cool that Nehemiah was a take-charge kind of guy. When I read chapter four, I saw that he was really good at motivating people to do the right thing. He just had the touch. I need to be that way for Jorge.

Luis

Real Question

How can you show Jesus' attitudes and life to your friends?

Who are the most influential people
in your life? Maybe there's a teacher you
admire, or an older friend, possibly your parents.
Whoever it is, we tend to model our behavior after
that person's lifestyle and choices. So, you can quickly see
from Jorge's example, that choosing the wrong role model—or
being a wrong role model—can lead to trouble. Jesus came to earth
not only to pay the price for our sins by going to the cross but also to
serve as a living example of how we are supposed to live (John 13:15).

How can Luis be like Jesus to his friends and Jorge? What words of
advice would you give to him?

Real Answer

Imagine the president of the
United States coming to your
house just to do a chore for you. Not
just any job—the worst one you have. As the
soon-to-be Savior of the world, Jesus definitely
outranked the president in importance. Yet, at the Last
Supper, he washed the dusty, undoubtedly smelly feet of
his disciples (John 13:1-11). A good host usually made sure that
his guests' feet were washed. But the host wouldn't do the job himself. This was a servant's task—and not a treasured one at that.

Why did Jesus do that? Jesus spoke of his action as an example to be
followed (John 13:15). He wanted his disciples to know that a true leader
is also a servant. That's why he also said, "The greatest among you must
be a servant" (Matthew 23:11). Does this mean we're on foot patrol with
each other? Not literally—unless you want to! It just means being willing
to do whatever it takes to help someone. In Luis' case, that means pro-
viding a positive alternative to drinking and hanging out. It means not
being too proud to take on a dirty job for a friend. It means being a leader
by example, not by orders or strength or peer pressure.

It means being like Jesus. He said, "Do as I have done to you" (John
13:15). What are you waiting for?

real you

Here are three ways I can
model Jesus to my friends
and family:

_____

_____

_____

_____

_____

_____

_____

_____

_____

_____

_____

_____

_____

_____

_____

_____

_____

_____

_____

_____

_____

_____

_____

_____

Here are three areas in my life that I need to change so I can better reflect Jesus' life and attitudes:

_____

_____

_____

_____

_____

_____

_____

_____

_____

_____

_____

_____

_____

_____

_____

_____

_____

_____

_____

_____

_____

_____

Xalted

Everlasting Light

Nothing quite like having a little
light when you're hiking on a dark trail.
Anyone on a trail with an unreliable light
source is headed for real trouble. The same is
true when we try to find our way through life without a reliable "light source." Jesus was sent to bring
light to a world of darkness. As a source of light, he's completely reliable. He'll never grow "dim." He'll stay "lit" for all eternity.
That's why he's the everlasting light (Isaiah 60:19-20).

I find the Jesus Experience when I am assured that there is life after death.

"There are many rooms in my Father's home, and I am going to prepare a place for you. If this were not so, I would tell you plainly."

John 14:2

reaL Xpressions

Too Young to Die

Several months ago, my best friend Dana died. The drunk driver who hit her car walked away without a scratch. There's something seriously wrong with that picture.

All I can think of are the things Dana never got to do—prom, driver's license, state gymnastics meet. And the more I think about it, the more depressed and angry I get.

For a while, I felt like I was completely falling apart. I couldn't stop crying. Dad said that was fine, though. He said I needed to work through my grief, no matter how long it took.

He also reminded me of all our good times together, like the time Dana and I dressed up like Siamese twins for a school spirit day, and the time we got sprayed by a skunk and spent the whole weekend trying to get rid of the smell. I kept thinking about all we'd done together, and for a couple minutes, I actually smiled.

Then Dad reminded me of the day four years ago at church camp when Dana and I both committed our lives to Christ. "Dana's life isn't over, Erin," he said, "Just her time on earth. As soon as she took her last breath, she was with God, in a place so incredible we can't even imagine it. She'll never experience pain, suffering, or sadness again."

At first I fought that idea. I refused to accept it. Even now, I'm not saying everything's magically OK. I still feel empty inside, like a part of me is missing. I miss her, and I always will. If I could change things and bring her back, I would. But there's some touch of comfort in knowing that God himself is taking care of her. Someday I'll see her again, and that's enough to keep me going for now.

Erin

REAL QUESTION

What really happens after we die?

The thought of death is one of the biggest fears people have. Death is "the great unknown." A lot of people aren't sure what happens afterward. After all, dead people don't usually come back to tell their stories on "Oprah." ("I see dead people—next on 'Oprah'!")

Yet one of the harsher realities of life is that people die, sometimes through tragic circumstances. These deaths cause people to lose hope. But is death the final frontier? Is there no hope of anything beyond it?

If you knew Erin, what would you say to her about Dana? How can a person really be sure about what happens after death?

REAL answer

After the death of his friend Lazarus, Jesus spoke some words of comfort to Lazarus's sister Martha: "I am the resurrection and the life. Those who believe in me, even though they die like everyone else, will live again. They are given eternal life for believing in me and will never perish" (John 11:25-26). Because Jesus died and was resurrected, he has ultimate power over death. Death is not the final end for each person. Those who trust Jesus as Savior will be resurrected just like him and go to live with him.

Years after Jesus' resurrection, the apostle John saw a vision of heaven. What he saw became the book of Revelation. God allowed him to catch a glimpse of heaven (Revelation 21–22). Imagine the most incredible place you've ever seen. Now imagine a place that's even more spectacular than that. Can't do it? Then check out John's vision. He saw a sparkling city "filled with the glory of God" (21:11). In heaven "God will live with [his people]. He will remove all of their sorrows, and there will be no more death or sorrow or crying or pain. For the old world and its evils are gone forever" (21:3-4).

Can you imagine that? No wars. No poverty. No hunger. No pain. No gangs. No terror. Heaven is a place where "nothing evil will be allowed to enter" (21:27).

John didn't just see a city. He also saw some of the occupants of that city. "I saw a vast crowd, too great to count, from every nation and tribe and people and language, standing in front of the throne and before the Lamb. . . . And [the angels] fell face down before the throne and worshiped God" (Revelation 7:9-11). This is one party that will never end.

You will spend eternity somewhere, either with Jesus or without. It's your call.

ReaL YOU

Some fears that I've had concerning death are the following:

_____

_____

_____

_____

_____

_____

_____

_____

_____

_____

_____

_____

_____

_____

_____

_____

_____

_____

_____

_____

Because of what I know about Jesus, this is what I can share about life after death with others:

_____

_____

_____

_____

_____

_____

_____

_____

_____

_____

_____

_____

_____

_____

_____

_____

_____

_____

_____

Xalted

Eternal Life

Some things seem to go on forever.
Exams. Boring lectures. Dental procedures.
But even they come to an end eventually. The
oldest person in the world has a life that seems to
have gone on forever. But that life eventually will end.
Jesus promises that those who trust him will have life that
will continue after death. Jesus not only promises it, he *is* it. First
Timothy 6:12 describes him as "the eternal life that God has given you."
That's a truth worth holding on to.

I find the Jesus Experience when I trust that he is in complete control.

"I have been given complete authority in heaven and on earth."
Matthew 28:18

REAL XPRESSIONS

The Shooting

Terrorists crashing planes into buildings. Anthrax. And now this. A kid I know at school, Justin, brought a gun to school and shot two sophomores. I always thought my senior year in high school would be the best year of my life. I was wrong.

A week ago, school finally seemed relatively normal. Everybody seemed hopeful again after the terrorist attacks. But all of that changed on Thursday. I had a weird feeling as I drove to school that day. I'm no prophet. I believe in Jesus and stuff. Maybe the Holy Spirit was warning me.

At fourth period, Justin suddenly appeared at school with a gun. I don't think I saw him earlier. Not that I keep track or anything. The guy's always been a little weird. He was on the wrestling team with me, but I still feel like I hardly know him. When the coach cut him from the team, I guess he decided to take it out on everybody else. Somehow he made it all the way to the coach's office. Coach must've been talking to the two sophomores at the time who had just made the team. Chris and Sean. Justin shot them before two guys jumped him. I wished I had been one of those guys.

Everybody freaked out. We were all sent home. On the way home, my girlfriend just couldn't stop crying. Watching Lynnae cry (and trying to watch the road at the same time) I suddenly realized that I was crying too. I didn't even know Chris and Sean that well. But what Justin did to them was almost like he did it to all of us.

I heard on the news that Chris and Sean survived. I thanked God for that. Justin tried to kill himself, but the police stopped him.

We didn't have to go to school the day after the shooting. Who would've wanted to? But when we did return, everybody was back to looking scared again. I admit this had me running scared. But one cool thing that came out of this was that the pastor of my church was invited to speak to the school. I guess the principal thought we all needed some counseling or something. He read Psalm 23 to us. Then he told us that God was always with us and was in control of all events. A lot of us were crying. I think we all needed to believe that God was in control.

Rich

Real question

When trouble comes, where is Jesus?

Have you ever been afraid that something terrible would happen? Some people fear being mugged, so they travel around with an arsenal of pepper spray and other weapons. Some are afraid to fly so they drive everywhere they want to go. Some are so fearful that they don't want to leave the safety of their homes.

Trouble comes in many forms. It can seem overwhelming at times. Within the last decade, some of the worst tragedies have occurred in schools. Who could ever forget Columbine—the site of the worst school shooting to date? Many walk away from these tragedies with a sense of hopelessness. Some have chosen to end their lives because they could see no way out of the despair. Others decided to be angry with God for allowing these horrors to occur.

If you had a chance to talk to the students at Rich's school, what would you say? How would you feel about school after an incident like this? How would you feel about God? Would it seem he is in control of all things?

Real answer

Before his death, Jesus had one last teaching session with his disciples. Some of what he said might have been hard to take: "Here on earth you will have many trials and sorrows" (John 16:33). He wasn't kidding. Within hours, a mob would come to arrest him. He would have to put up with a grossly unfair series of trials before being condemned to one of the most painful deaths imaginable. God allowed his own Son to be put to death for crimes he didn't commit. The disciples would later experience persecution and death. Hard times were coming!

But with the bad news came the good: "I am leaving you with a gift— peace of mind and heart. And the peace I give isn't like the peace the world gives. So don't be troubled or afraid" (John 14:27). "Take heart, because I have overcome the world" (John 16:33). Before he returned to heaven, Jesus assured his disciples with these words, "I have been given complete authority in heaven and on earth" (Matthew 28:18).

Jesus is completely in control of all events in your life and his promise is this, as the apostle Paul wrote, "And we know that God causes everything to work together for the good of those who love God and are called according to his purpose for them" (Romans 8:28). That doesn't mean God promises we'll like everything that happens to us, or that we'll understand everything that comes our way. But we can be confident that God is in control and will work everything out according to *his* good purposes.

In the midst of tragedy and death, there is hope. This hope is centered in Jesus. He gives believers the power to hang on even through great tragedy because we know he's taking care of business.

Want to know where Jesus is when trouble comes? He's right there with you. In control of every situation. Trust him.

Real You

It's hardest for me to believe
Jesus is in control when I see
the following events take place:

_____

_____

_____

_____

_____

_____

_____

_____

_____

_____

_____

_____

_____

_____

_____

_____

Because of my trust in Jesus, I'm counting on this promise he has given:

_____

_____

_____

_____

_____

_____

_____

_____

_____

_____

_____

_____

_____

_____

_____

χalted

Commander of the Lord's Army

Some of the evil we experience in our world is part of an ongoing spiritual battle. God is on one side and Satan is on the other. Every army has a leader. Jesus is the commander of the Lord's army (Joshua 5:14-15). All authority has been given to him. Although wars and death at times make Satan look like he's winning, Jesus promises that the final victory belongs to him.

I find the Jesus Experience when I place my security in what's eternal.

"Don't store up treasures here on earth, where they can be eaten by moths and get rusty, and where thieves break in and steal. Store your treasures in heaven, where they will never become moth-eaten or rusty and where they will be safe from thieves. Wherever your treasure is, there your heart and thoughts will also be."

Matthew 6:19-21

real Xpressions

A Poor Investment

I live in a big house in an expensive neighborhood. I drive a car that most 17-year-olds only dream about. I've already been accepted into an Ivy League school.

I know. Poor me, right? You don't know the half of it. See, we're broke now. I'm not sure what my family will do. It's all because of my uncle—my mom's youngest brother, Allan. My mom trusted him to invest our money. (My dad's dead.) If you can't trust your own brother, who can you trust? Well, in less than a year, he not only lost most of our money, he used some of it to cover up on some bad investments he made for others. He might have to do jail time because of that.

The court froze all of our assets. Our house and my car will be sold to pay off some of our debts. I could hardly believe it when Mom told me the news. No wonder she's been looking worried for the last six months or so. She hasn't been able to even look at Uncle Allan. I don't think she'll ever forgive him. I know I have a hard time doing that.

I've always felt so secure because we had money. I never thought anything like this would happen. Mom says that maybe this is how life was like during the Great Depression. (It's not like she'd know for sure. She hadn't been born yet! *Her* mom hadn't even been born!)

I guess my dad was right. See, my dad was a Christian. He kept telling my mom that we shouldn't base our security on money. Instead, we should put our hope in God. None of us wanted to listen to him. I only went to church because Dad wanted us to go. My mom went for the same reason. When he died a year ago, I stopped going. It's not that I didn't believe in God. It's just that he wasn't important to me. Now my mom is thinking about going again and wants me to go too. I guess it takes a disaster to bring you back to God.

Catherine

REAL QUESTION

Is God against people having money?

What's your image of Jesus? Someone who walked around without a cent to his name? Someone who barely had one outfit to put on? Maybe you've read the story in Mark 10:17-25 about the rich young man who approached Jesus. He wanted to know how to gain eternal life. Jesus told him to "Go and sell all you have and give the money to the poor, and you will have treasure in heaven" (Mark 10:21). Maybe that has made you feel guilty about all the stuff that you have. Maybe you've wondered whether you're expected to give away all that you own. Most people would say that idea has all of the charm of a football player taking ballet.

More than likely, you've heard that "money is the root of all evil." That's actually a misquote of 1 Timothy 6:10. Still, this verse caused a lot of people to wonder whether God wants everyone to be poor. What do you think?

Many people depend on assets like money. All is well if they have the gold. Sadly, that's why many people ended their lives after the Stock Market Crash of 1929. When the economy failed, they couldn't go on. Does having money help you feel secure? What is Catherine's fear? How would you feel if you were a member of her family?

REAL ANSWER

Jesus had more to say about the topic of money than about anything else. During his Sermon on the Mount (yeah, he preached a while up there) Jesus gave some advice about money. He knew that money was one of the things that people worried about. Worry sometimes caused people to hoard money or items that were worth money. So he said, "Don't store up treasures here on earth, where they can be eaten by moths and get rusty, and where thieves break in and steal. Store your treasures in heaven, where they will never become moth-eaten or rusty and where they will be safe from thieves. Wherever your treasure is, there your heart and thoughts will also be" (Matthew 6:19-21).

In other words, putting your trust in money is a bad idea. You might have twenty pieces of valuable art that you think will see you through any hard times. But suppose they were stolen or a fire broke out? That's why Jesus wanted people to see that heaven—having a solid relationship with God—is a better investment. Does that mean money is evil? No. "The *love of* money is at the root of all kinds of evil" (1 Timothy 6:10). Greed—the desire to keep acquiring money, money, money—is the problem.

Jesus knew that people who based their whole lives on the money they made were actually servants of money. "No one can serve two masters. For you will hate one and love the other, or be devoted to one and despise the other. You cannot serve both God and money" (Matthew 6:24).

Neither of the two states (having money or not having money) is the preferred one. As one proverb writer put it: "Give me neither poverty nor riches! Give me just enough to satisfy my needs. For if I grow rich, I may deny you and say, 'Who is the Lord?' And if I am too poor, I may steal and thus insult God's holy name" (Proverbs 30:8-9). In other words, be content with what God gives you.

Real you

As I think about money, I've always felt most secure when:

_____

_____

_____

_____

_____

_____

_____

_____

_____

_____

_____

_____

_____

_____

_____

_____

_____

Knowing Jesus is going to provide for me helps me make these decisions about money:

_____

_____

_____

_____

_____

_____

_____

_____

_____

_____

_____

_____

_____

_____

_____

_____

_____

_____

_____

_____

_____

_____

_____

Xalted

Prince

Know any princes? Many countries with monarchies have them. A prince isn't a prince without a kingdom. The prophet Ezekiel said the Messiah would become a "prince among [his] people" (Ezekiel 34:24). That description refers to Jesus (see also Acts 5:31). While on earth, he preached about his kingdom—the kingdom of God. This is one kingdom you can count on to never disappear or disappoint. It's not based on power, wealth, or military might. Rather, it's based on who knows and accepts the one, true King.

I find the Jesus Experience when I place my security in the family of God.

"Pray like this: Our Father in heaven, may your name be honored."

Matthew 6:9

REAL Xpressions

Deep Wounds

The day that Dad moved out, Mom had made a big dinner, as usual. Dad had been coming home late most nights. We believed him when he said that work had been really busy. We really didn't suspect anything—at least I didn't. I guess Mom stayed up a lot of nights worrying. She'd felt distant from him, but still she tried to believe the best in him.

So we were pretty much blindsided when he said that he was leaving. He told Mom there was someone else. That was enough to make me want to disown him. He never said a formal good-bye, just left. He'd been so busy with "work" that he hadn't spent much time with me in months. Mom was absolutely crushed. All I felt was rage.

How could he do it? After 18 years together—building the house, working through grad school, raising me, going to church, teaching Sunday school—how could he throw it all away? Dad's Christian reputation was ruined, and rightly so.

Mom's small group pulled together around Mom and me. They checked on us all the time, to make sure we were doing OK. I guess it's times like these when you really learn who your real friends are. There's no doubt that what the Bible describes about adultery is right. By being unfaithful, Dad destroyed our family. He burned himself. He wounded us. I can't help but feel so bitter toward him. Mom is holding us together somehow. Even when I don't feel like it, we pray together every night. She says that my Heavenly Father will never fail me.

Andrew

ReaL QueSTIon

Is any family really secure
these days?

What was the biggest fear you had
when you were younger? Think waaaaaayyy
back. For many kids, the biggest fear was that
their parents would divorce. A sad fact of life today
is that more than half of all marriages fail. You probably
have a number of friends whose parents have divorced.

For many, the family is the most important aspect of their
lives. It's their security in an unfriendly world. They work hard to keep
their family together. If it were to fall apart, their whole world would
crumble.

How secure is Andrew's world right now? How does Andrew feel about
his dad? How would you feel if you were Andrew? Does his experience
mean that you can never really count on your parents?

ReaL answer

One of God's com-
mandments was to honor
parents (Exodus 20:12; Ephesians
6:1-2). However, he knew that we
humans often fail each other. Yet, through
Jesus, we now have access to his Father, the one
who will never fail us.

Jesus often spoke about a Father who is known in the
Old Testament as a "Father to the fatherless" (see Psalm 68:5).
This father was God, the first member of the Trinity. When he taught
his disciples about prayer, he invited them to address God as their "heavenly Father" (Matthew 6:9; Luke 11:2). Not only that, he referred to God
as *Abba,* an Aramaic word for *Father* (Mark 14:36). That was pretty radical! The Israelites never would have presumed to think of God as a dad!
But to Jesus, God wasn't just "Father." He was "Daddy." That meant he
had an intimate relationship with God.

Because of Jesus, we can have that relationship with the heavenly Father.
Years later, the apostle Paul said, "So you should not be like cowering, fearful slaves. You should behave instead like God's very own children, adopted
into his family—calling him, 'Father, dear Father' " (Romans 8:15).

God is like the ultimate Super Dad. You can be sure he'll never walk out on you! He promises never to leave nor forget his people, "'I will never fail you, I will never forsake you.' That is why we can say with confidence, 'The Lord is my helper, so I will not be afraid. What can mere mortals do to me?'" (Hebrews 13:5-6).

That's one father you can always count on.

Real you

I have certain expectations of my family. Some of these are:

_____

_____

_____

_____

_____

_____

_____

_____

_____

_____

_____

_____

_____

_____

_____

_____

_____

_____

_____

_____

Knowing that I can call God "Daddy" makes me feel like this:

_____

_____

_____

_____

_____

_____

_____

_____

_____

_____

_____

_____

_____

_____

_____

_____

_____

_____

_____

_____

_____

_____

_____

_____

_____

XALTED

Mediator

If you have an argument with someone, do you ever wish you had a mediator? This is someone who represents your side of the argument. Jesus is the mediator between God and human beings. (See 1 Timothy 2:5 and Hebrews 12:24.) Because he is both God and man he is uniquely qualified for the job. Because of his sacrifice on the cross, we have the right to call God "Father."

Day 30

I find the Jesus Experience when I really believe that God will never reject me.

"But now I am going away to the one who sent me, and none of you has asked me where I am going. Instead, you are very sad. But it is actually best for you that I go away, because if I don't, the Counselor won't come. If I do go away, he will come because I will send him to you."

John 16:5-7

real Xpressions

A Tough Transition

I never expected it would be easy to transfer to a new school, but I didn't think it would be this tough. I just transferred to this prep school six months ago at the beginning of my junior year. It's supposed to be this amazing school that will automatically get me into any college I want. Yeah, that's the speech my parents gave me. ("Dylan, this is for your own good.") I don't disagree with that, but the transition has been miserable. So far, I don't have any good friends in this place.

Sometimes I feel like a leper. It's like all the friendships are set in stone around here. I've tried to meet people. I even talked to a couple of guys in my homeroom about hanging out over the weekend. (I haven't had the nerve to ask out a girl yet.) One of them said he had something to do. I tried to shrug it off by saying, "Oh, no big deal." Yeah right. That makes rejection #250. The other guy told me about some big party he was going to. (That's probably what the first guy had going on, too.) Of course, the new kid wasn't invited. That hurt. See what I mean about feeling like a leper?

At least God hasn't rejected me. I keep a card in my locker that has one of my favorite verses on it. It says that God's eyes search the whole earth to strengthen those who are committed to him. I pull that card out all the time. Sometimes I really need it!

Transitions can be hard, you know? It's tough being left out at school. I never expected everything to run perfectly when I arrived at this school, but I had hoped it wouldn't be this difficult to make friends.

I'm glad God cares about how I feel. He doesn't want me to sit around feeling sorry for myself, but at least I don't have to pretend with him that everything's cool.

Dylan

Real Question

How are we supposed to deal with rejection?

Have you ever felt rejected? You're not alone (even though it feels that way). Most people have felt rejection at some point. It really stinks. Most of us would do anything possible to avoid it. That's why the fear of rejection is so powerful. No one wants it!

Think about a time when you felt like Dylan. What were the circumstances? Did anything make you feel any better? If you've never experienced the feeling of being left out, imagine yourself in Dylan's shoes right now. What Bible verse would you look at for comfort? If you knew Dylan, what would you do or say to encourage him?

Have you ever known anyone who went along with the crowd because he or she feared rejection? Maybe he or she did things to keep the crowd's approval. But how long do you think that approval lasts?

Real Answer

Jesus can relate to rejection. Many of his people rejected him. He was constantly misunderstood or viewed with suspicion. The Pharisees once accused him of using Satan's power (Matthew 12:22-32). That was the worst thing they could have said to him. His hometown of Nazareth even rejected him! (See Mark 6:3-6.)

His treatment was foretold in the book of Isaiah. "He was despised and rejected—a man of sorrows, acquainted with bitterest grief. . . . He was oppressed and treated harshly, yet he never said a word" (Isaiah 53:3, 7). Still, knowing this didn't make the rejection easier to take. But Jesus knew something else: that he was greatly loved by God.

This love, and the knowledge that he had a mission to accomplish, helped him to persevere.

Jesus knew too, that his followers would face rejection and far worse treatment because of him. His followers today still face persecution and rejection because of their faith. So are we left on our own when times of rejection come? Not at all. Jesus promised his followers that when he left them, he would send another, a comforter, a counselor, a friend, who would always be with them and never leave them (John 16:5-7). That friend? The Holy Spirit—the same one who is promised to all believers throughout the ages to bring us comfort, guidance, and encouragement.

Jesus knew exactly what his followers needed when he walked the earth. He still does.

When you face times of loneliness and rejection, remember you can turn to the one who is always there. He understands. He's there to help. "The LORD keeps watch over you as you come and go, both now and forever" (Psalm 121:8).

ReaL You

This is a time when I faced rejection. This is how I handled it:

_____

_____

_____

_____

_____

_____

Because Jesus understands and has sent his Holy Spirit, I can do the following when facing rejection:

_____

_____

_____

_____

_____

_____

_____

_____

_____

_____

_____

_____

_____

_____

_____

_____

_____

_____

Xalted

Angel of the Lord

Have you ever wondered what an angel looks like? The Bible is full of instances where an angel delivered an important message or protected someone. Before coming to earth as a man, Jesus was thought to have appeared during Old Testament times as the "angel of the Lord." He appeared at times of great despair or challenge to people like Abraham, Hagar, Moses, and even to a donkey owned by a disobedient prophet! (See Numbers 22:21-35.) If you trust Jesus as your Savior, you don't need to wait for an angel to appear. You've got God himself living with you!